P9-CQA-965

REINVENTING FUNERAL SERVICE

VOLUME I. PRODUCT MERCHANDISING

ALTON F. DOODY, JR., Ph.D.

Chairman and Founder
The Doody Group
New Orleans, Louisiana

Formerly Professor of Marketing
The Ohio State University
Columbus, Ohio

Center for Advanced
Funeral Practice Management

Center for Advanced
Funeral Practice Management

International Standard Book Number: 0-9639580-0-3

Library of Congress Cataloguing-in-Publication Data:

Doody, Alton F.

Reinventing Funeral Service

1. The Doody Group. 2. Funeral services industry—United States.

This book is available at a special discount for bulk purchases for educational use. For details contact:

Special Sales Director
Center for Advanced
Funeral Practice Management
3701 Canal Street
New Orleans, Louisiana 70119
504-488-9500

Printed by Fine Line Graphics, Inc., Columbus, Ohio.

Printed in the United States of America.

Dedication Page

To My Mother and Father

Althea Leitz Doody

and

Alton Frederick Doody, Sr.

CONTENTS

ACKNOWLEDGMENTS

Many years ago, I discovered that the science of merchandising is based largely on probability theory. Oversimplified, it is the proposition that sales goals are met by exposing enough products and/or services to enough people.

So it is with life's experiences. Six years ago when I was first introduced to funeral service, I did not know that I would become so heavily involved in the death care industry or that I would meet so many interesting people. But once I got involved—I should have known—it was the law of probability theory. One thing leads to another.

My association with the industry began with the Batesville Casket Company. The Batesville management group—especially Dave Hirt, Ken Camp, Tom Crawford, and Mike Ertel—patiently supported new merchandising concepts long before they became proven plans and programs. And Dan, Gus and John Hillenbrand consistently have been supportive from the corporate level.

I have been associated with so many people at Batesville that I couldn't possibly name them all here. I would like to because many have become good friends. But the names Randy Salatin, Doug Gober, Rick Green and Dan Reukauf must be recognized individually—Randy as Corporate Director of Merchandising; Doug, Rick and Dan as top professional sales representatives, with a wealth of experience about merchandising in their own right.

These men were handpicked to work with me as a task force to study every aspect of casket merchandising. We started with ideas, formulated these into concepts, then developed test applications, which subsequently became industry-wide programs.

It was at Batesville that I met Jerry Pullins, then President of The Sentinel Group and now, Senior Vice President, Corporate Development, SCI. Jerry quickly recognized the value of the new programs under development and asked me to become a Director of his company to assist him with implementation.

At Sentinel, I met Dillis Ward, Frank Sessions, Valarie Wages, John McGilley, Mark McGilley, Mike Devaney, Richard Hoffmeister, Bill Branson, Bob Pisano, and John Anderson. Each of these individuals gave wholehearted support to the early installations even though there was nothing to go on but floor plans and illustrations.

It was as a result of my move back to New Orleans in 1989 that I met Jerry Alexander of Stewart Enterprises, Inc. Jerry gave generously of his time to make me feel welcome in the city and, in turn, introduced me to Frank Stewart and the senior management group of Stewart Enterprises, Inc., including Larry Berner, Rick Baldwin, David Clayton, Ron Patrone and Bill Rowe.

Once again, one thing led to another. The Doody Group's first assignment was the complete remodeling of the Lake Lawn Metairie Funeral Home. This led to being chosen for the design and development of their new funeral home—the All Faiths Funeral Home. This, in turn, has led to projects for Stewart in Alabama, Florida, Maryland, Tennessee and Texas.

To refine the programs under development, I turned to old friends and associates—Denny Riga, Lajos Szabo, Sr., and Lajos Szabo, Jr., my partners in Applied Retail Systems.

Their work on layouts, fixtures, signing and other aspects of selection room design was pioneering in character and their recent work on modularly constructed selection rooms has been distinguished.

I also must recognize the highly original contribution of Mary Fox Linton and Gavin Johnson Stuart, world class designers from London, England, who developed the color and interior concepts that have been so successful in funeral home installations throughout the country. Assisting in this effort from the beginning were my wife, Betsy Doody, and Gail Schmidt, who undertook the original field survey research.

I want to recognize in a special way, my associates in The Doody Group. Cindy Cruikshank has helped me turn ideas into working drawings and working drawings into completed funeral homes. Cindy's skills as a professional designer and as a superb contract manager have been invaluable. Lynn Taggart, with twenty years of retail merchandising experience, has helped me refine and interpret the principles of assortment planning and store design as they apply to funeral products.

Finally, I want to thank my administrative assistants, Joy Huntley and Sally Lawton, without whom this book could not have been written. Joy skillfully managed my office during much of 1993 so that I could devote the time to prepare this manuscript.

Sally has been my research and writing assistant on the project from its inception in the summer of 1992. Sally actually made this project fun. Her computer and grammar expertise is such that the manuscript was written in real time—no sooner would I generate an idea than she would have it back to me for further work. I already have decided that I don't want to write any book without her help.

—AFD

INTRODUCTION

As the millennium approaches, funeral service certainly will change dramatically along with every other aspect of our society.

This book is for those in funeral service who are greatly concerned about the business and the profession, because their life work has been in this field and because they know the satisfaction of serving people at a time when they are in great need.

This book is for those who sense that change is *positive.* It is for those who have glimpsed that there are better ways of doing things—even dramatically better ways of doing things—but have not yet put these into action plans and programs.

It is for the *seekers*, the *unsatisfied*—not for those who are comfortable with the present.

If ever there was a time for seekers, it is now. New laws and regulations are governing funeral service, new competitive structures are emerging and, most important of all, new consumer attitudes and values about funeral service are requiring us to do things quite differently. But this is not all bad or a threat; it is the opportunity for tomorrow!

Reinventing Funeral Service tells us about such opportunities. But it does not deal with trivial matters—it deals with the bold steps needed to transform our businesses in order to be prepared for the twenty-first century. As is so eloquently pointed out, this means giving up some of our past practices and doing some things differently—and doing some new things. I shall not forget the admonition: "We must avoid doing better things that we shouldn't be doing at all!"

It is a particular satisfaction for me to write this introduction as I have had the pleasure of knowing Dr. Alton F. Doody personally since he moved back to his native city, New Orleans, some five years ago.

We are kindred spirits. We share a love for New Orleans. We serve on the Tulane Freeman School of Business Advisory Council together. We are both members of an old, revered Mardi Gras club. But, most important, we share an intellectual curiosity about discovering ways to improve funeral service.

I write this Introduction knowing that the ideas and principles put forth in this book really work! With the help of Alton Doody and his talented associates in The Doody Group, I have put them to use in our company—for the benefit of the customers we serve, for my associates, and ultimately, for our stockholders.

—Frank B. Stewart, Jr.
Stewart Enterprises, Inc.
New Orleans, Louisiana

WHY THIS BOOK

Have you ever known anyone with a thyroid deficiency?

If you have, then you are aware that perfectly normal and balanced individuals—with energy, enthusiasm, ability, drive, and determination—can be stopped dead in their tracks, sometimes to the point that they are barely able to function day to day.

Once diagnosed, due to the miracles of modern medicine, individuals with this condition can take a minuscule, low-cost pill each day which brings their metabolism back into balance, so that they can go forward and lead perfectly normal lives again.

I have written this first volume of what is to become a series of books on funeral service simply because I believe that I have uncovered the equivalent of the "thyroid pill" for this industry. And, like the medical analogy referred to above, the actions that need to be taken are modest in scope, low in cost, and low in risk.

I am referring to the fact that funeral directors—being primarily service providers—do not really know very much about the product or the merchandising side of their businesses, at least from a professional planning perspective.

My background, on the other hand, is not that of a funeral director, but that of a professor of marketing and a professional merchandising consultant. It was in this capacity that my firm was retained by the Batesville Casket Company to review marketing and merchandising practices in the industry. I became fascinated with the industry. The primary reason was that I saw a direct application of well-established marketing and merchandising principles that could be applied to most funeral operations—bringing about immediate and dramatic improvements—for the benefit of ultimate consumers and funeral home operators alike.

In my career, which now spans several decades, I have had the opportunity to work with successful consumer goods manufacturers and retailers throughout the world. I am proud of the work that I have done and that my various companies have done for such firms as Ford, Mazda, RCA, Lévi Strauss, Wal-Mart, Target Stores, Kmart, and many others.

But not all of our work was done for large companies. Through vendor-sponsored programs, such as Ace, Cotter and HWI, we were able to work with thousands of retail hardware and lumber dealers. Through franchise programs such as IGA, 7-Eleven, and Rexall, we were able to work with supermarkets, convenience stores, and drug stores.

Our success, like any company, was measured by our growth and financial performance. But, in the final analysis, it was measured by the pragmatism and the operational relevance of our ideas and concepts. That is, to what extent did our know-how and our recommendations really work?

I believe that we always scored high marks in this regard. We were the first consulting group to recognize the emergence of the discount department store and the discount specialty store as dominant distribution mechanisms in the American economy and, subsequently, the world economy. We developed pioneering store planning, layout, and design concepts that were the basis for new store formats throughout the world. We developed merchandise assortment, fixture, presentation and pricing strategies that significantly improved the productivity and profitability of such firms as Wal-Mart on the one hand, and the Mainstreet Hardware Store on the other.

But *nowhere* in our professional experience have our recommendations, designs and formats produced anything like the dramatic results that we have achieved in the funeral services industry! Here, we are not improving product assortments by 5%, 10%, or even 20%; we are going for 30%, 40%, 50% and even 100% improvements! Here, we are not looking for small, incidental increases in productivity and profitability, but quantum jumps. Here, we are not thinking in terms of actions which will produce a 20% to 30% return on new investment, but a 100%, 200% and even 500% return on incremental investment!

Hence, the title of this book, ***Reinventing Funeral Service*, Volume I. Product Merchandising**. As you will see, the process of reinventing, reengineering, restructuring, and reinvesting is not about bringing about small, incidental improvements in running a business. It is about finding the *key elements* of the business that can be changed in ways to completely transform the business, to make it into the next generation enterprise serving consumers, employees, and owners in the most satisfactory ways possible. It is the process of true innovation, of real revitalization and renewal.

I have written this book because funeral service can be—*it must be*—more than it is at this time, if it is to fully serve the needs of society in the twenty-first century.

—*Alton F. Doody, Jr.*
New Orleans, Louisiana

CHAPTER 1

THE REINVENTING • REENGINEERING • RESTRUCTURING • REINVESTING PROCESS

A ROAD MAP FOR DRAMATIC CHANGE

Reinventing defined: The process of ***dramatically*** changing one or more of the key variables in a business to produce ***radically superior*** results.

In my book, *Reinventing the Wheels*,[1] I describe how the Ford Motor Company put together a turnaround strategy in the early 1980s that became the model for the American automobile industry. Chrysler embraced this strategic approach in the mid-1980s and, finally, General Motors did so in the early 1990s.

[1]Alton F. Doody and Ron Bingaman, *Reinventing the Wheels: Ford's Spectacular Comeback*. (Cambridge, Massachusetts: Ballinger Publishing Company, a subsidiary of Harper & Row, 1988).

Ford's experience, however, transcends the automobile industry. The company pioneered a *process* that all companies, large and small, can follow in the future as they reinvent, reengineer, restructure, and reinvest in themselves in order to adapt to the *new realities* of the marketplace in the 1990s and beyond.

The process produces curious anomalies and paradoxes. In Ford's case, it produced vastly superior cars from a quality, dependability and customer satisfaction viewpoint, but did so with far fewer manhours of assembly time and at dramatically lower overall cost. Concurrently, it created real partnerships with production workers and with vendors for the first time in U.S. auto manufacturing history and it produced the highest profits in the history of the company.

How could this happen? How is it possible to produce more with less? It all started in 1979 when Philip Caldwell, Ford's newly appointed CEO, recognized that the company was bloated, burdened, and unwieldy. Caldwell knew that the company could do better, indeed, that it had to do better. Manufacturing quality was at such a low level at Ford in 1979 that the company actually recalled more cars than it produced! The overall financial situation was so precipitous that Ford lost $3.26 billion between 1979 and 1982. Getting things turned around was not an easy task. In the 1979-1982 period, seven huge manufacturing facilities were closed and 101,000 jobs were removed from the payroll.

Does this sound familiar in the 1990s? In the last five years, General Motors has lost $30 billion and has reduced its workforce by 25%—almost 200,000 jobs lost. IBM has lost $18 billion and has cut its workforce almost in half—from 405,000 to 225,000 jobs. Sears has lost $3 billion (from its merchandising operations) and has reduced its workforce by almost a third—100,000 jobs lost. Perhaps you remember, as I do, when these companies were thought of as the paragons of managerial and business excellence. Yet, in a little more than a decade, they have gone from being world class leaders to caricatures of their former selves.

What did they fail to do? In essence, they failed their customers–they failed to offer products, services, prices and values that were as good as their competitors'. And, interestingly, when the troubles began with these great companies, they perceived their competitors to be merely upstarts! What was Toyota or Honda compared to General Motors? What was Microsoft or Dell Computer compared to IBM? What was Wal-Mart or Home Depot compared to Sears?

In the Sears case, I have some personal experience. My consulting company was invited to assess the retailing challenges facing Sears in the 1980s. We already had identified the rapid growth of the discount department store format and had predicted that this would be the dominant form of retailing for ordinary, everyday, general merchandise products in the future. We cited the rapid growth of Kmart, Target, and Wal-Mart (companies that we had actually worked with) and explained the power and the logic of their self-service, central checkout, shopping cart approach to merchandising. We pointed out the subtleties of the new approach whereby "self service"–for easily recognized, branded products–was not *less service*, but actually *more service* in that the customer could shop at his or her own pace, rather than being dependent upon a sales clerk. And we pointed out that *self* service didn't mean *no* service, but better service because the sales persons who were on the floor could be more efficient and effective.

I remember vividly the specific example used and the discussion that ensued between a senior officer of Sears and me. I had made the comment that a woman buying two gallons of paint at Sears–carrying out one in each hand–was "closed to buy" any other merchandise on the same shopping trip because of the weight and bulk of the products. I contrasted the purchase process at Sears with that of Kmart or Wal-Mart whereby the customer would select the paint, put it in a shopping cart, continue purchasing all other needs, pay once at the checkout counter, and then take all of the products in the shopping cart to the car. My point was that this needed to be thought of as *more service*, not *less service*. The Sears' executive defended his company's approach and mentioned that his company offered a "will call" service, whereby customer purchases were taken by employees to a special drive-up waiting area. A polite but somewhat heated discussion ensued, as I remarked that "this was trying to do better something that shouldn't be done at all!" In the first place, it was high cost compared with the self-service checkout approach, and secondly, it required extra effort on the part of the store employees and customers, who oftentimes had to wait in a will-call line behind other customers just to pick up purchases.

I have frequently thought back on this meeting. Our observations and our recommendations fell upon deaf ears. I think it was a pity that we failed to communicate more urgently and more effectively. Perhaps we could have steered Sears in the right direction, avoiding the catastrophe which has subsequently befallen it. At the time of this meeting in 1980, Sears' sales were ten times greater than Wal-Mart's! Today, less than 15 years later, Wal-Mart's sales are twice those of Sears'!

I remember a similar encounter with the senior management group of a large and prestigious hotel chain. At the time, this company operated over 50 hotel properties in major cities throughout the United States. It was a leader in the hospitality industry. Holiday Inn, Ramada, and other "motel" companies were merely "upstarts."

The discussion at hand was about the growing acceptance on the part of consumers for motels rather than hotels. At the time, almost all hotels were in "prime" downtown locations. They provided doormen, bellmen, room service, restaurant service, and valet service. Motels, in those days, were in "secondary" suburban locations and offered few, if any, of these amenities.

With the benefit of hindsight, of course, we know that the motel *reinvented* the lodging industry by meeting the needs of contemporary travellers. It was a creative response to the growing importance of the automobile, the highway, suburban development, family travel, casual lifestyles, permanent-press clothing, and many other factors. The downtown hotel, on the other hand, was actually a creation of a former era. It flourished when people traveled by train, dressed and acted more formally, and when most guests were travelling executives or salesmen.

For the modern age, the motel did not offer less, it offered more. The "more" did not include doormen, bellmen, room service, and fancy restaurants. The "more" was free parking, free carts to assist with luggage, free ice, convenient, inexpensive vending machines and free swimming pools.

Actually, the hotel executives were more responsive than the Sears executives. A baseline study was commissioned to document trends in the hospitality industry. Some actions were taken to make some of the hotels more responsive to the new competition. But, in the final analysis, management failed to take the decisive steps that were necessary to transform the company. It stubbornly clung to its old format until its profits turned to losses and the properties had to be sold off one by one. Today, this company is out of business.

I have always felt that this was a fascinating aspect of the business decision process. As a general rule, business people get so caught up with what they are doing that they fail to grasp the sweep of change and the need to do things differently.

I don't know whether it will be any different in the funeral services industry. But, the purpose of this book is to define the issues and to identify the key variables that can change, to better serve consumers, better serve employees and better serve owners.

At this point, you may be thinking—this is all quite interesting, but how does this apply specifically to funeral service? After all, funeral service is a very stable and traditional business. Things actually don't change that much in this business!

Nothing will jeopardize your business more in the future than to hold to such a view! I'm writing this book out of the conviction that the above proposition is entirely *false.*

First, a review of Howard Raether's landmark work, *Funeral Service: A Historical Perspective,*[2] reveals that funeral service in America has changed rather dramatically over the years. Actually, funeral service has been reinventing itself all along!

But today, the pace of change is quickening. There is the new challenge of publicly-financed, corporate-owned funeral home chains, the growing power and importance of cemetery/funeral home combinations, aggressive pre-need sales organizations, well-entrenched cremation and burial societies, and perhaps, right over the horizon, a type of funeral service business will provide the consumer with a new interpretation of "more for less."

In addition, the visible terrain of change suggests that the very *nature* of the service-product offer that is provided by funeral service will change in this decade. Firms that understand this change and embrace it will be the ones that thrive and prosper. Those that do not will be severely disadvantaged. This is the case simply because the new ways are better ways—they make it possible to reinvent, reengineer, restructure, and reinvest.

[2]Howard C. Raether. *Funeral Service: A Historical Perspective.* National Funeral Directors Association, 1990.

Just as the science of jet propulsion totally transformed the airline industry in the 60s and 70s, and the science of quartz crystals totally transformed the watch industry in the 70s and 80s, the *science of merchandising* will totally transform the funeral service industry in the 1990s and beyond. This may sound like an outlandish statement. But if you will read on, I believe that I can convince you that this is the case beyond a shadow of a doubt.

This transformation, based upon a totally professional approach to the merchandising of *all* product categories associated with funeral service, will happen, first and foremost, because it serves customers more fully. Greater choice is at the center of the modern consumer movement. More and more, Americans are demanding products that meet *precisely* their *individual* perceptions of what they need and want.

This transformation will serve funeral arrangers more fully by making it *easier* for them to assist customers. Sound merchandising programs and properly planned selection rooms make it possible for customers to better determine their real needs, not relying as much on the arranger's verbal or spoken explanations.

This transformation will serve owners more fully by providing the cash flow and profits needed to reinvest in the business to support new levels of service, new types of service, superior locations, superior facilities, more effective employee training programs, improved employee benefit programs, and finally improved profitability.

The decision to apply advanced merchandising principles to the funeral services industry will *not* be optional. This is because major innovations—when they truly produce superior results—force all firms in an industry to move in the new direction. This was certainly true for aircraft manufacturers, who were forced to abandon piston engine planes for jet planes, and for watch manufacturers who were forced to abandon mechanical-geared movements for electronic quartz movements.

In the final analysis, it is a matter of economics. It is a matter of marginal returns versus marginal costs. In the case of funeral service—as will be seen in the pages that follow—the marginal returns are extraordinarily high. The marginal costs are relatively low and the risks are commensurately low. This makes the decision process—in the vernacular of today's generation—a "no brainer."

CHAPTER 2

REINVENTING
YOUR TOTAL MERCHANDISE OFFER

Everybody wants a better product. *Companies should give it to 'em!*

—*Ely Callaway*
Callaway "Big Bertha" Golf

Gone are the days of one size fits all. Consumers are *demanding* and *getting* an ever more specialized response to their needs. Just take a look at the salad dressing section of your supermarket the next time you're there. Or take a look at the cereal section. Remember when there were just Corn Flakes and Cheerio's?

—*Michael Sorrentino, President*
Donghia Furniture & Textiles,
Steelcase, Inc.

My work in funeral service began inauspiciously enough. In 1987, I was asked by the Batesville Casket Company to critique the merchandise reporting system that the company had developed for its key customers.

Batesville, as a leader in the industry—postulated as far back as 1974—that there must be a way to apply retail merchandising and display principles to the casket sales aspect of funeral service. To this end, the company invested considerable resources.

In 1975, an elaborate experimental showroom was designed, constructed, and installed in Batesville's Cincinnati Service Center. This was a large space—approximately 3,000 square feet in size—with revolving turntables, indirect lighting and dramatic, almost theatrical displays.

Batesville also developed its "Merchandise Analysis Reporting System," available to customers as a service at no cost, to help funeral home owners and managers fine tune the sales and profitability of their casket assortments. A noteworthy aspect of this reporting system was the development of the merchandise "kite," which showed the need for planning an assortment above and below the average unit sale of the firm. A feature of the reporting system was the year-end sales and profit analysis which assisted the funeral home owners and managers in planning and projecting their casket assortments and pricing for the following year.

While the Batesville merchandising reporting system had been successfully adopted by some 2,000 firms, the company realized that this was a mere 10% utilization factor given that there are some 20,000 funeral service establishments in the United States. My initial assignment was to familiarize myself with the industry and recommend ways in which the reporting system might be improved and how its benefits might be communicated to funeral directors more advantageously.

Funeral Home Visits

In order to do this, it was necessary for me to get out and visit a representative sample of funeral homes around the country. I did this with the full cooperation and the gracious hospitality of funeral home owners everywhere.

Altogether in my initial study of the industry in 1987 and 1988, I visited over fifty funeral homes—some in metropolitan areas, some in smaller cities and some in rural areas. I visited very large firms, such as Rose Hills in Los Angeles and Restland in Dallas; intermediate sized firms, average sized firms, and small firms. I visited firms with new facilities, recently remodeled facilities, and others that were very much in need of doing over. I visited cities with very few funeral homes per 1,000 population, such as Richmond, Virginia and Columbus, Ohio, and cities with many funeral homes per 1,000 population, like Buffalo and Albany, New York. I visited firms serving primarily the white middle-class market, serving the African-American market and still others serving the Hispanic market with its various subsets—Cuban, Puerto Rican and Mexican. I also visited firms catering to particular religious or ethnic groups, such as Orthodox and Asian.

I will never forget my overall impression from these visits. From a *merchandising management viewpoint* it is as if I had walked into a time capsule! Here was an entire industry operating in the 1980s at the level of retail merchandising of the 1880s; kind of on par with the old general store!

To be sure, some of the physical facilities were beautifully and elaborately furnished, and some of the selection rooms were attractively "decorated"—with new carpet, wallpaper and the like—but from a professional *planning* point of view, product assortments were limited, product adjacencies did not exist, product pricing was confusing to the consumer, product displays were poor, traffic patterns and layouts were cumbersome, and, consumer information—as imparted through price lists and/or signs—was at a low level.

I would like to describe to you in detail my impressions from these visits:

Casket Merchandising

With regard to casket merchandising, the funeral home owner or manager typically would choose, on the basis of a sales call from a manufacturer's representative, 15 to 20 units that he or she thought families would purchase. The caskets would arrive at the funeral home to be placed in a large rectangular room, typically 1,000 to 1,500 square feet in size. With the exception of an "explanation grouping" sometimes found at the front of the room, caskets would be dispersed almost at random throughout the room. This means that a bronze casket could be next to a 20-gauge steel casket, which in turn could be next to a cherry hardwood casket, which could be next to a 16-gauge steel casket, which could be next to a copper casket, which could be next to a cloth-covered casket, and so on.

Exclusive of New England, New Orleans, and a few other special markets, almost all of the units on display were of metal. A room with 20 caskets, for example, would usually have 17 metal caskets and three wood caskets. The breakdown of the metal assortment might include a single bronze casket, two or three copper caskets, and 12 to 14 steel caskets. The breakdown of the wood caskets might include a mahogany casket, an oak casket, and a poplar or a pine casket.

During the course of my visits, I asked funeral home owners and managers what they thought the ideal number of caskets should be in the selection room. The answer I received almost invariably was the number of caskets shown on the floor—15 to 20 units. We would discuss larger assortments, but these were felt to be confusing to the shopper and impractical from a space point of view. And, of course, they were right—given the fact that there was no logic applied to the placement of the caskets to begin with. If the customer preferred copper, he/she had to "wade' through the other products on the floor. If the customer preferred wood, he/she had to search carefully for the meager assortment that was available. Keeping in mind that under every circumstance this is not a "fun" shopping experience—that the customer doesn't want to be there to begin with—this is a serious matter.

When asked about the metal/wood split—80% to 90% metal and 10% to 20% wood—the characteristic reply would be: "We don't really get many calls for wood—most of our clients prefer metal."

Item identification and price signing tended to be very limited, if done at all. Most establishments relied primarily on printed "price lists"—showing casket prices from the most expensive to the least expensive, cross-referenced to the name and model number assigned by the manufacturer.

When price signs were employed, they were found placed on the bed of the casket, generally as a typed or printed card. Occasionally, metal price signs were used, placed in the bed or on the closed lid of the casket.

Casket displays consisted of various types of pedestals—ranging from simple plexiglas stands to ornately decorated wood and metal biers. Oftentimes, more than one kind of pedestal would be used in the same room. A number of selection rooms employed double racks. These were mostly of two types—racks with an undercarriage so that the lower casket rolled out for opening and inspection, and high rack frames featuring both units open, with the top unit on an angle so that the interior of the casket is visible to the buyer.

In terms of design, decor and lighting, casket selection rooms ranged from attractively appointed rooms to those that had been sadly neglected for many, many years. There were, unfortunately, more of the neglected rooms than there were well-done rooms. I found this to be surprising in view of the importance of merchandise sales to the overall profitability of funeral home operations.

Other Funeral-related Products

Other funeral-related products—vaults, children's caskets, clothing, urns, monuments, markers, and flowers—were handled in such diverse ways that it would be almost impossible to generalize. I cannot help but state, however, that the overall impression was not pleasing or particularly helpful to the customer.

Vaults sometimes were located within the casket selection rooms—sometimes not. Vaults tended to be sold from miniature scale models, but on occasion, they were sold from full-sized units. Some featured composite concrete vaults and metal vaults, others handled only one of the two materials.

In some funeral homes, clothing was housed inside the casket selection rooms and in others outside. In some cases, clothing was on display and other times it was kept in closets. Almost invariably, however, it was kept in plastic dry-cleaning type bags.

Urns were displayed in casket selection rooms in some establishments and in arrangement rooms in others. Urn assortments ranged from a few items to a large number and urn display fixtures ranged from attractive, bookcase-like displays to dilapidated and rickety shelves.

Owner/Manager Perceptions

On certain aspects of merchandising—most notably vendor choice, number of caskets to be carried, and markup practices—funeral home owners and managers had *strong opinions*—even though they were diverse. Some owners, for example, tended to concentrate purchases with a few vendors. Others were fearful of this practice and bought from many vendors. Some priced conservatively—such as a 2.0 times markup; others marked up as high as 4.0 to 5.0 times.

When queried about merchandising practices, some funeral home owners made reference to the fact that they are on the "Copper Approach," the "Value Approach," the "World Program," the "VAS" program, the "FSA" program, or the "Package Merchandising Program." Detailed discussions of these programs oftentimes revealed very obtuse perceptions about the merchandising objectives of these programs.

On other aspects of merchandising—such as product assortment, layout, design, decor, lighting, and display—I didn't get any sense of a "correct" approach. The idea of standardized formats, color schemes, display fixtures or signing just didn't seem to be regarded as important.

Overall Assessment

In trying to develop an overall assessment of this situation, I would constantly try to put myself in the *mindset of the consumer* trying to make a buying decision based upon what I was observing. In doing so, quite frankly, I had a sense of bewilderment, confusion, and sometimes even revulsion. A subsequent review of industry survey research and focus group studies reveals that many consumers have the same feelings.[3]

[3]Ernest Morgan. *Dealing Creatively with Death: A Manual of Death Education and Simple Burial.* (Bayside, New York: Barclay House, 1990), pp. 46-49.

There just has to be a better way! Fortunately, there is. It involves applying well-established, proven merchandising and retail planning principles to the funeral services industry.

MERCHANDISE MANAGEMENT IN FUNERAL SERVICE

In my textbook, *Retailing Management*,[4] the subject of merchandising is covered in detail. In fact, the merchandise management section consists of eight separate chapters, 207 pages, representing a full third of the book. To fully capitalize on this body of knowledge, funeral home owners should appreciate that there is an organized, systematic body of knowledge on this subject. Those who grasp this knowledge and apply it to the funeral service business will be at a considerable advantage over others in the years to come. After all 50% to 60% of a funeral homes' total revenue comes from the sale of funeral-related products.[5]

The term "merchandising" can be defined as: "The planning involved in marketing the *right assortment* of products, at the *right price*, at the *right time*, in the *right quantities*, in the *right environment*."[6]

[4]William R. Davidson, Alton F. Doody, and Daniel J. Sweeney. *Retailing Management.* Fourth Edition. (New York, John Wiley & Sons, 1975).

[5]To arrive at the percentage, 50 to 60%, it is necessary to include product sales that are handled by funeral homes on an agency basis, such as vaults and monuments. Technically, in some funeral home accounting systems, vault sales, monument sales, and some other lines of products are not treated as "sales" but as "commissions earned" or "other income." The important fact is that funeral homes derive substantial revenues from these product lines. They are a basic part of the "economics" of the funeral service business. In this sense, they should be thought of as sales. This is in contrast to "cash advances," which are typically handled without a markup.

[6]Davidson, Doody, et al. *Retailing Management,* page 171.

The Scope of Funeral-related Products

The merchandising planning process begins with a consideration of the lines of products and items that a funeral home *could offer* to its customers. A comprehensive listing of such products is as follows:

Caskets/Containers

- Metal (sealing models and non-sealing models)
- Wood
- Fiberglass
- Cloth Covered
- Oversize
- Youth/Infant
- Orthodox
- Cremation Caskets/Containers
- Shipping Containers
- Custom/Special Order Caskets

Vaults/Outer Containers

- Composite Concrete
- Metal
- Plain Concrete
- Wood

Clothing/Shrouds

- For Men
- For Women

Monuments/Markers/Lettering

- Marble/Granite
- Composite
- Cast Bronze
- Cast Aluminum
- Combinations

Insignias/Flags/Memorializations

- To be placed on caskets, monuments or markers
- To be retained by the family, e.g., flags, register books, photographic memorializations, video/audio memorializations
- To be presented to visitors, e.g., memorial cards, memorial service booklets
- To be given as gifts, e.g., ecclesiastical vestments, religious objects, and the like—to churches or ministers in memory of the deceased

Cremation Urns
- Metal
- Wood
- Ceramic/crystal/glass
- Marble/granite
- Composite
- Plastic/paper
- Combinations of the above

Flowers
- Fresh cut
- Dried
- Artificial

Flower Vases for Gravesites and Mausoleums
- Marble/granite
- Metal
- Other

The purpose of the itemized list is to suggest to funeral home owners and managers the *range and scope* of the merchandising opportunity presently existing in the industry. Ideally, from a merchandising point of view, a well-run funeral home would offer for sale *every item* on the list, except for those that are inappropriate for one reason or another due to local conditions or state regulations. In New Orleans, for example, vaults are rarely used. In some cities, vaults are sold only by cemeteries. At most "memorial park" type cemeteries upright monuments are prohibited in major sections of the cemetery. Obviously, in such cases, product assortments should not include such items.

The Merchandise Management Process

The merchandise management process is to: 1) establish solid vendor relationships that guarantee continuity of supply; 2) plan meaningful product choices for consumers; 3) price clearly but profitably; 4) create superior merchandise displays; 5) utilize good sales support materials, and 6) present product choices in a complimentary, supporting environment. A corollary challenge is to accomplish all of the above in a way that does not complicate the business beyond its manpower, space, and financial resources.

Quite obviously, not every funeral home should handle every product listed above. In the broadest sense, however, this is the challenge—to better serve consumers by providing as full a range of products needed or desired in connection with a death, a funeral, a burial, a cremation, or a memorialization of a loved one.

VENDOR RELATIONSHIPS

Developing a sound merchandise program begins with the recognition that funeral homes do not operate in a vacuum. Modern merchandising is too complicated and time consuming.

Sophisticated merchandisers seek out solid vendor partners who provide not only products, but *total systems* supporting the products. These systems might include advice on building an assortment, model stock "planograms," pricing programs, displays, fixtures, stock replenishment systems, extended credit terms, seminars on advanced merchandising practices, point of sale support materials, and many other formal and informal types of assistance.

It is interesting to observe how few funeral homes take full advantage of the support systems that have been developed in the industry. There seems to be a fear of relying too heavily on vendors. This results in quite a lot of "episodic" buying rather than systematic buying.

Ironically, smaller funeral homes are more prone to this than the large firms. I have my own theory about the reasons why. Smaller firms, perhaps, have longer periods when they are slow. Interviewing salesmen is one way to pass the time when this happens. Unfortunately, however, when unplanned, casual purchases are made, it disrupts the overall merchandise plan and jeopardizes the potential profit goal.

Keep in mind that sophisticated retailers—firms like Wal-Mart, Toys "R" Us and Home Depot—have abandoned the old style of buying and have moved aggressively toward long-term, key vendor programs. In fact, Wal-Mart's new store in Rogers, Arkansas has been planned in total cooperation with key vendors. The logic behind this store is that the vendor knows many things about the product line and the market for the product line that the retailer doesn't. Therefore, the vendor needs to plan, in conjunction with the buyer, the optimum assortment, the ideal price points, the most professional fixtures and displays, the replenishment system, and otherwise provide full support for the line in order to maximize sales and profits.

The extent and sophistication of such programs is appreciated when it is recognized that reordering is now *automatic*; it is a by-product of the planned assortment. The mechanics are accomplished through "EDI"—Electronic Data Interchange—whereby the retailer's point of sale computers are linked directly to the vendor's computers, making for "paperless" purchasing and invoicing. Quite obviously, such programs would not work if there was not a definitive, agreed-upon merchandise plan.

It is only a matter of time before such systems are available in funeral service. This will greatly simplify ordering, accounting and bookkeeping, and will make merchandise reporting and analyses an automatic spin-off of the system. It will also lower costs in an industry that has experienced cost creep in recent years—whereby operating expenses have been rising faster than prices for services or for merchandise.

MODEL STOCK PLANNING

Once a determination has been made regarding the vendor partners that will supply you with product, it is possible to go to the second step in developing a professional merchandise plan; namely, to determine the specific lines that you are going to handle and the specific items that you're going to make available for sale—either directly or through a third party, as may be the case for vaults, monuments, flowers, and the like. In retailing, this is called *model stock planning.*

In funeral service, certain categories of product tend to be purchased directly from manufacturers at wholesale. The funeral home buys these products, takes title to them, inventories them and resells them to the consumer. Caskets, clothing, and urns are examples of such products. Other categories tend to be sold by display sample on an agency basis, such as vaults, monuments, markers and flowers. Of course, there are exceptions to the above. A number of larger funeral homes operate their own flower shops. A number of combination cemetery/funeral home operations buy monuments and markers and resell them to ultimate consumers.

Regardless of these technical differences, there are tremendous improvement possibilities available to apply modern merchandising principles to the products of this industry.

Model Stock Planning for Caskets

While the opportunity for greater service to consumers and greater profits to the firm are possible from *all* of the product lines cited above, developing a clear and balanced model stock program for caskets is far and away the most important single thing that a funeral home can do. In fact, given the "economics" of the funeral home business, casket merchandising probably is more important to profitability than all other categories combined.

Accordingly, the subject is covered in detail in this analysis. More effective casket merchandising, in the context of a fully developed model stock program, is at the very center of reinventing, reengineering, restructuring, and reinvesting for the future.

When I first began my study of this industry, I was struck immediately by the serious *mismatch* between the breadth of line that the manufacturer produced and the skimpy assortments that were offered to consumers by funeral homes.

Casket manufacturers, as a group, produce well over 2,000 distinctly different caskets in the United States. In retailing, we refer to these distinct differences as SKU's, which stands for stock keeping units. Batesville manufactures some 600 units when all factors are considered—material, gauge, color, hardware, shell shape, finish (brushed, painted, shaded) full couch versus half couch, type of interior, design of interior, and color of interior. Aurora manufactures some 900 units, as does York. The preceding numbers, incidentally, do not consider products that are made specifically different by using a cap panel or by some other special color or feature produced as a custom casket.

Let us assume for the moment that the average funeral home in the U.S. displays and stocks 20 caskets. What this really means is that the average funeral home utilizes less than *one percent* (1%) of the output of the industry! When you stop and think about it, I am sure that you will agree that any system operating in this manner is enormously high in cost and wasteful.

I do not know a single other consumer products industry that operates in this fashion. Can you imagine a Ford dealer stocking only one or two models of the Ford line and keeping his franchise? Can you imagine a GE appliance retailer offering ten to twelve different washing machines, but only one or two clothes dryers?

Yet, this is roughly analogous to what happens in funeral service when a decision is made to feature metal caskets and almost ignore wood caskets or when a decision is made to stock almost all steel caskets and only a few semiprecious metal caskets. From the beginning of my work in this industry, I have been frustrated by the *gap* that exists between what the manufacturer produces and what the funeral home displays. To put the matter simply—most funeral homes have inadequate, *anemic* assortments!

What then, is an adequate assortment or a complete and balanced model stock? It is one that truly satisfies your customers' needs and wants—allowing them to choose from a reasonable and representative output of the industry. It is one that offers different styles, designs, colors, materials and price points to satisfy individual preferences—whether they be philosophical, psychological, religious, aesthetic or economic.

How did the industry come to hold the view that an ideal casket assortment ranges between 15 to 20 units to accommodate "at need" sales and 12 to 15 units to accommodate pre-need sales sold from a brochure? As far as I can tell, the overriding consideration has been fear of confusing the customer.

This brings us to one of the most fundamental questions of this book: *Is the problem of confusing the customer a function of the* ***number*** *of caskets being offered? Or is it a problem of* ***organizing, classifying*** *and* ***displaying*** *the caskets being offered?* I submit to you that the problem is *not* the former, but the latter.

Organizing the Stock

How then, do we go about organizing the stock to create an adequate, consumer-satisfying assortment? We do this by structuring the stock in *the way that most consumers want to buy*! And, in funeral service, the first decision is one of expressing a preference for material—almost always metal or wood. It follows, therefore, that our casket assortment must be displayed by having all of the metal caskets together and all wood caskets together.

Classifying the Stock

Beyond organizing the stock (metal versus wood), it is necessary to *classify* the stock in a way that further helps the consumer make an intelligent buying decision. It is here that we create "worlds," applying the *good–better–best* principle. For most funeral homes serving a broad market, this would be to classify the steel world as "good"; copper/stainless as "better," and bronze as "best." Likewise, pine and poplar would be classified as "good"; cherry, oak and maple as "better"; mahogany and walnut as "best."[7]

Using the above as criteria, it would follow that the basic parameters of a model stock for a "typical" funeral home serving a broad middle market might be as portrayed as in Exhibit A.

EXHIBIT A A MODEL STOCK OVERVIEW FOR A "TYPICAL" FUNERAL HOME SERVING A BROAD MIDDLE MARKET	
METAL CASKETS	
BEST	BRONZE
BETTER	COPPER/STAINLESS
GOOD	STEEL
WOOD CASKETS	
BEST	MAHOGANY/WALNUT
BETTER	CHERRY/MAPLE/OAK
GOOD	PINE/POPLAR

It is important to understand that the *principle* of developing a model stock does not always correlate to this *particular interpretation* of good–better–best.

In an inner-city low-income market, for example, where the average sale might be $1,000, the model stock might be interpreted quite differently, as shown in Exhibit B.

[7]It is recognized that wood caskets sometimes are made from other specie—such as pecan, ash, birch, and fir—and that veneers and cloth-covered caskets are an integral part of the industry. It is also recognized that fiberglass caskets are manufactured and sold in the industry. It is only necessary to substitute or add these products to the appropriate classifications when they apply.

EXHIBIT B A MODEL STOCK OVERVIEW FOR A INNER-CITY FUNERAL HOME SERVING A LOW INCOME MARKET	
METAL CASKETS	
BEST	COPPER AND/OR STAINLESS
BETTER	16-GAUGE/VELVET
GOOD	18/20 GAUGE/CREPE
WOOD CASKETS	
BEST	CHERRY/VELVET
BETTER	POPLAR/VELVET
GOOD	CLOTH COVERED

This is nothing more than Saks Fifth Avenue applying the principles of model stock planning differently than Wal-Mart. The *principles* are the same; it is the customer base and the merchandise choice that is different.[8]

Customer Choice

The next step in model stock planing is to provide *your* customers with a *range of choice* in each classification that is meaningful to them. In most funeral homes—serving a broad market—this would mean having a bronze assortment of three to five units, a copper and/or stainless assortment of six to eight units, a steel assortment of eight to ten; a walnut/

[8]In funeral service, it is widely recognized that choice of casket—by quality and price—does not correlate precisely with traditional socioeconomic classifications. For example, upper-income consumers are not necessarily the best purchasers of the finest caskets. But it is possible that funeral home owners and managers have exaggerated these differences. After all, buyers of better merchandise, in the final analysis, must have the purchasing power to make better quality commitments.

mahogany assortment of three to five units; a cherry/maple/oak assortment of six to eight units and a poplar/pine/cloth-covered assortment of eight to ten units, as is portrayed in Exhibit C.

EXHIBIT C
A MODEL STOCK UNIT PLAN FOR A "TYPICAL" FUNERAL HOME SERVING A BROAD MIDDLE MARKET

CLASSIFICATION (WORLD)	PRODUCT TYPE	DESIRED RANGE OF UNITS
METAL CASKETS		
BEST	BRONZE	3-5
BETTER	COPPER/ STAINLESS	6-8
GOOD	STEEL	8-10
WOOD CASKETS		
BEST	MAHOGANY/ WALNUT	3-5
BETTER	CHERRY/ MAPLE/OAK	6-8
GOOD	PINE/POPLAR	8-10
TOTAL CASKETS		34-36

In anticipation of your raised eyebrows . . . . Yes—I am aware that this adds up to 34 units on the low side and 46 units on the high side and that your initial impression is that this is way too many.

But is it really? Probably not—*if* you put yourself in the position of the *consumer* trying to make an important purchase—one that is charged with emotion, taste preferences, and financial significance.

In retailing parlance, we would call this type of purchase a "shopping good" purchase rather than a "convenience good" purchase. That is, it is a *significant* purchase; not an incidental purchase. It is a purchase that is worthy of effort—to evaluate alternatives, appropriateness, features, and prices. In other words, it is a "big ticket" purchase. I often remind funeral directors that casket prices *begin* where refrigerator prices leave off!

Consumers are not passive participants in the trend toward greater product choice in the American society. *They are driving it.* They are demanding wider choice in order to achieve a *deeper fit* with their lifestyles and values. They are no longer satisfied with mere *fundamental variety*, they require *peripheral variety* as well.

The range of products on the market as a result of this trend is staggering when compared with two decades ago. Consider for example, the number of items carried in a supermarket today with the number twenty years ago. Bakery items have increased by 1,753%, beverages by 1,111%, breakfast cereals by 1,350%, and dairy products by 1,735%. This trend is documented in detail in Exhibit D, shown on the following page.

For automobiles, the trend is the same. In 1960, there were 19 brands of cars on sale in the American market and 78 basic models. In 1990, the number of brands had increased to 38 and the number of models had increased to 283, as indicated in Exhibit E.

EXHIBIT D
INCREASED PRODUCT AND BRAND CHOICE IN SUPERMARKETS
SELECTED CATEGORIES OF CONSUMER GOODS, 1970-1991[9]

CATEGORY	1970	1991
BAKERY FOODS	93	1,631
BEVERAGES	123	1,367
BREAKFAST CEREALS	8	108
CANDY, GUM, SNACKS	195	1,885
DAIRY	64	1,111
PET FOOD	36	202
SOUPS	12	265
HEALTH & BEAUTY AIDS	201	3,064
PAPER PRODUCTS	31	165
PET PRODUCTS (NON-FOOD ITEMS)	2	74

[9]Source: Secondary research survey conducted by Strategic Information Services, Inc., Columbus, Ohio, 1992.

EXHIBIT E
INCREASED NUMBER OF AUTOMOBILE BRANDS AND MODELS
IN THE AMERICAN MARKET, 1960-1990[10]

CATEGORY	1960	1990
NUMBER OF BRANDS	19	41
NUMBER OF MODELS	78	283

[10]James P. Womack, Daniel T. Jones, Daniel Roos, and Donna S. Carpenter, *The Machine That Changed the World.* (New York, New York: Macmillan Publishing Company, 1990).

But you remain skeptical! You are not yet convinced! Perhaps I can anticipate your objections.

You may be thinking, "This is fine theoretically, but it isn't practical . . . . I simply don't have the space to show that many units." Certainly space is an important limiting factor. But chances are that you have more space than you think! You probably are not using your space *productively* at this time. Fortunately, new selection room planning, display and fixturing techniques have been developed that will *greatly expand* your existing capacity. This important topic is taken up in detail in the Chapter 4 of this book.

You may be concerned about the investment required to carry such a large assortment. Indeed, for the typical funeral home to go from a conventional assortment of 15 to 20 units to one that adds 10, 15, or even 20 units, more money will be tied up in inventory. An analysis of this subject is reserved for Chapter 5, which deals specifically with profitability and return on investment. Suffice it to say at this point that the incremental investment is modest when related to the potential return.

Finally, to allay your skepticism, the ideal assortment—34 to 46 units—may not be ideal for you. There are still some geographical markets that have such a strong preference for metal or wood that it would not be correct to balance the model stock on a straight 50-50 metal-wood split. Because of this, your overall assortment might be reduced somewhat. However, it is more desirable to err on the high side than the low side, as full assortments enhance customer satisfaction, enhance funeral arranger effectiveness and increase your profit potential.

NAMES AND NOMENCLATURE

As you know, the prevailing practice in the industry is to rely on manufacturer names and model numbers when referring to a particular casket, as for example: "Y-33, Silver Rose." This is fine for wholesale ordering purposes, but it is not a good idea from a *retail merchandising* point of view. It can project a confusing image to the consumer.

Keep in mind that the individual names assigned to caskets by manufacturers have evolved down through the years. This means that they are not necessarily in sync with the *position* that you desire that casket to play in your particular assortment. From a retail merchandising standpoint, there needs to be a *relationship* between the name used and the status of the casket in the assortment.

As a general rule, names assigned to high-end units should be descriptive of high-end places or personages, such as President, Monarch, Senator, Congressional, or the like. Names assigned to middle-priced units, should be descriptive of fine things or places, such as Bentley, Carlton, Carlisle, Hyde Park, or the like. Names assigned to lower-priced units should be more nondescript, such as Fairlane, Abbey, Huntley, or the like.

You may think of this as a trivial matter. But it is just one of the many dimensions of model stock planning that distinguishes the professionals from the amateurs, the winners from the "also rans." Further, when you stop and think about it, of what possible relevance is a designation such as Y-33, Z-64, X-51, etc., etc., to an ultimate consumer? This is merely one more example of how easy it is for all of us to fall into a *trade-oriented focus* when we need to have a *customer focus.*

To make matters worse, manufacturer names sometimes can be awkward or even downright offensive to the consumer, such as "Tigereye" or "The Last Supper." They can also be *misleading* to the consumer. A "Sierra Bronze," for example, is not a bronze casket at all; it is a bronze-colored casket. This is not a problem from a wholesale point of view. Everyone associated with funeral service knows that this manufacturer's product is an 18-gauge steel casket. It is not that the manufacturer deliberately set out to mislead the consumer. This name, no doubt, was chosen to make a descriptive statement at a certain point in time, probably to compete directly with a competitor's casket. It is confusing, nevertheless, for the consumer to see the word "bronze" used in this context.

Another reason to avoid using manufacturer product names is to avoid direct price comparisons between your funeral home and that of your immediate competitors. Obviously, the most popular casket models and styles tend to be handled by more than one funeral home in a given market. Since it is unlikely that you will have exactly the same price as your competitor, you can avoid the matter altogether by assigning your own names to the merchandise that you sell. This is perfectly legal and ethical in most states and there is no Federal Trade Commission requirement at this time for you to utilize the casket manufacturer's name on your price list or on your signs. You are free to call a casket by whatever name you wish.

MODEL STOCK PLANNING FOR OTHER FUNERAL-RELATED PRODUCTS

The model stock approach outlined above is based upon well-established *principles* and proven merchandising *practices* that have been used by successful retailers for decades. It follows, therefore, that they are applicable to the merchandising of all funeral product categories.

In total, there is as much of an opportunity to enhance the merchandise effectiveness of these categories as there is for caskets. Based on my personal observation, I would have to state that the average funeral home does not do any better a job of assortment planning, pricing, fixturing, or displaying of these lines than they do with caskets. If anything, conditions are more haphazard and random owing to the fact that these lines, on an individual basis, are not at present very important to the funeral home. The one possible exception is the sale of vaults.

The key to the effective merchandising of these "other" product lines is to develop model stocks, based upon solid, consistent and *programmed* relationships with the suppliers. From the funeral home operator's point of view, this could be an easier task than for caskets as many of these lines are sold from display samples rather than from inventory. This opportunity, of course, is directly related to the professionalism of the assortments and the displays. Because of this, further discussion of these product categories is reserved for Chapter 4, which deals with selection room planning—traffic circulation, fixturing, merchandise capacity, merchandise presentation, display, lighting, and environmental enhancement.

CHAPTER 3

REINVENTING YOUR PRICING STRATEGY

Madame, . . . the ribbon is free!

—Emile Zola
The Ladies Paradise

My favorite story about pricing is an incident described in Emile Zola's famous novel—*The Ladies Paradise*.[11] It is about a Parisienne who had purchased a special dress from the Ladies Paradise—the world's most famous department store of the time—to wear to a garden party hosted by Napoleon III.

She could not find a "ready made" hat that was exactly right with the dress, so her hatmaker offered to make one for her. Much to her amazement, he did this in her presence in just a few moments' time. He merely looked at the dress; took several pieces of fancy ribbon in his hand—made a tie

[11]*The Ladies Paradise* was the name used in the novel. The actual name of the store is the "Bon Marché," which operates to this day.

here, a knot there, added small pieces of lace and a veil, and voila!—he created the perfect hat for the occasion.

The lady was positively delighted and expressed her pleasure. But when she went to pay, she was surprised by the price and exclaimed something to the effect, "Mais, Monsieur, it is but several petite pieces of ribbon!"

With that, the hatmaker took his creation—made a pull here, a tug there—and the beautiful hat fell back into its original pieces. He then placed the ribbon into the lady's hand and said, "*Madame, the ribbon is free!*"

Pricing, of course, is as much of an art as it is a science. Funeral directors instinctively appreciate this and price their services accordingly. When it comes to the pricing of products, however, funeral homes have a tendency to use a pseudoscientific approach which is positively bewildering to the consumer.

If your funeral home is typical of those I have visited around the country, there is a tremendous opportunity to do a better job of pricing—once again for the benefit of the customer, for the arranger, and for the funeral home itself.

This chapter will show you how to integrate pricing techniques and policies into your overall model stock plan.

Approaches to Pricing

There are two fundamental approaches to the pricing of products. The first is the "cost-plus" approach and the second is the "selling-price" approach.

As the name implies, cost-plus involves adding a "markup" to product cost to a arrive at a selling price for each product. The selling-price approach assesses competitive conditions and then makes a judgmental determination of what you should charge for each product. It is *implicitly* based upon markup because the amount of the selling price, on average, must produce the dollars that you need in your business to cover your costs and earn a profit. However, it is a more flexible approach in that specific prices are *smoothed* to avoid awkward prices that do not have meaning to the consumer.

At present, most funeral homes rely too much on an exact cost-plus approach. This produces undesirable results. For example, if an item is to carry a 2.5 times markup, a casket costing $609 would retail for $1,523. A casket costing $927 would retail for $2,317.

This approach to pricing results in a large number of idiosyncratic prices, such as $1,523, $1,613, $1,642, $1,691, $1,953, $2,106, $2,317, $2,756, $3,207, $5,412, and so on. When I have asked about the appropriateness of this odd-number approach to pricing, the typical funeral home owner or manager replies something to the effect: "Caskets always have been priced this way . . ." or, "It gives the impression that we are very careful and precise in our pricing."

In truth, this is unnecessarily confusing to the consumer. More importantly, such odd prices *do not reflect a logical progression of value.* This can be corrected by applying the principles of price lining and price pointing to the funeral services industry.

Price Lining

An integral part of model stock planning is to make certain that the items tentatively selected fit correctly into price lines and into specific price points that are appropriate for your business.

Price lining is a way of thinking about your sales by major categories. It is a planning technique (looking forward) to anticipate results and an analytical technique (looking backward) to measure results achieved.

To fully understand this concept, it may be helpful to use an example from outside the funeral services industry. Brooks Brothers, as a fine clothing store, has three price lines for men's suits.[12] The top price line is "Own Make" ($600 to $900) featuring suits that have been made, until recently, in its own workrooms. These suits are made from the finest wools or worsteds and have a considerable amount of hand-tailoring in them. The second price line is known as "356" ($400 to $600) featuring well-tailored suits with many of the subtle features of the Own Make. A very large part of Brooks Brothers' total unit volume is sold within this price line. The lowest price line is known as "Brooksgate" ($200 to $400). Suits sold here are good quality garments, representing what the retailer feels is good value for the price. These suits are durable and serviceable, but they are almost entirely machine made. Many of these garments are sold to younger men.

Thinking in terms of price lines helps you position your model stock in the market and evaluate your specific prices compared to competition. It is simply one more check to see that you are where you want to be.

Referring again to our "typical funeral home" serving a broad market, the price lines in Exhibit F are representative of what might be practical. In actuality, of course, the price lines would vary somewhat in different parts of the country and in different competitive situations.

There is no hard and fast rule that the *spread* within each price line be the same. In the case above, the low price line has a spread of $1,500, the middle of $1,750, and the high has a spread of $3,250.

[12]Over time, due to inflation or as a result of a change in merchandising strategy, price line brackets will change.

EXHIBIT F PRICE LINES FOR A "TYPICAL" FUNERAL HOME SERVING A BROAD MIDDLE MARKET	
LOW PRICE LINE	$500 - $2,000
MIDDLE PRICE LINE	$2,000 - $3,750
HIGH PRICE LINE	$3,750 - $7,000

Price Pointing

Once the price lines have been ascertained, it is easier to complete the development of your model stock plan by *pricing your specific items* in a *logical progression of value* to the ultimate consumer. This is illustrated in Exhibit G shown on the following page.

In this specific model stock plan, note that all caskets in the Lowest Price Line have ended in $95; those in the Middle Price Line have ended in $75, and those in the Highest Price Line have ended in $50 or an even dollar number ($00). This is *not* a hard and fast rule, but there is logic to this approach. In the case of the lower-priced caskets, we want the psychological benefit of the $95 instead of $00 because research has shown the buyers really do think that an item ending in $95 as less than the one that has been rounded up to the next even number. Further, we probably need all of the margin that is available on lower-priced units.

In the case of merchandise that is priced in the mid-price line, we want to reflect a somewhat different posture to the consumer. Historically, in retailing, "better" merchandise has not been priced as close to the next highest rounded number (such as $95 or $99). Therefore, we have priced our better merchandise to end in $75. High-priced merchandise tends to be priced at a rounded number or at a price midway between two rounded numbers. Thus, in our example we have shown the high priced items to end in $00 and in $50.

EXHIBIT G SPECIFIC RETAIL PRICE POINTS REFLECTING A LOGICAL PROGRESSION OF VALUE	
LOW	$495 995 1,295 1,495 1,695 1,895
MIDDLE	$2,175 2,375 2,575 2,775 2,975 3,275 3,575 3,775
HIGH	$4,250 4,750 5,500 7,000

It is not necessary to price any casket below the $50 mark, such as $1,723. This is because a well-planned model stock—in the eyes of the consumer—has only *meaningful price differentials in a logical progression of value*. In casket merchandising, these are in the range of $200 to $300, except with highest priced items, where the differential is greater. What is of utmost importance is for the consumer to see and to perceive the *differences in value* between the different price points. These differences, of course, might be differences in material, in shell shape, in gauge, in hardware, in interior, or in the type of finish (brushed versus shaded versus painted).

The highest priced casket(s) on the floor (and on the price list) should end in an even number. This makes it easier for the consumer to mentally divide and perceive value at "half" the highest priced unit and the second highest priced unit. In our example, the highest priced unit is positioned at $7,000. Note that there is a price point at $3,575—about half of the highest price. We also have *coverage* in our assortment immediately above and below this price—$3,275 and $3,775. The second highest priced unit is $5,500. Note that there is a price point at $2,775—about half of this price. We also have coverage above and below this price—$2,575 and $2,975.

A model stock assortment plan developed in this way for our "typical" funeral home would likely produce a *modal* or middle average sale somewhere around the $2,375 price point. It would likely produce an arithmetic *mean* average sale around the $2,575 price point owing to the weighted influence of sales above this price. Quite naturally, the exact averages would vary from one establishment to another.

Keep in mind that there are likely to be *fewer price points* than there are items in the assortment. This is as it should be. The most popular price points should feature more than one item.

Stratospheric Pricing

I am frequently asked about the advisability of featuring an extremely high priced casket on the selection room floor or on the price list. There are arguments in favor of this. It certainly establishes a high starting point for the floor or for the price list. If it is on the floor, it also tends to feature a unit that is strikingly different from other items in the assortment, dramatically reinforcing the notion that the wide range in casket prices is directly related to the materials and workmanship of each unit.

There are arguments against having such an extremely high-priced unit in the assortment or on the price list. Funeral service has its share of critics. Some consumers, no doubt, would view an extremely high-priced casket to be inordinately excessive. As one funeral director commented on this topic: "I wouldn't think of having a $15,000 casket (at retail) on my floor. I don't want to look ridiculous to my friends or to my community!"

Market Positioning

In the final analysis, it boils down to *market positioning*. Who are your customers? How do you want to be perceived by your customers? Are you in a relatively homogeneous market or are you in a diverse market? These are questions that you must answer before finalizing your model stock and your pricing policy.

The general rule is to set your floor with highest priced units that are no more than two times the price of other units that you consider to be interesting to the consumer. In other words, products that can actually be sold in reasonable quantities. This involves engineering your highest priced bronze caskets to have a value relationship to one or more key copper caskets and your highest priced mahogany caskets to have a value relationship to your best cherry caskets. You engineer your next highest priced bronze unit to have a value relationship to better stainless steel and/or 16-gauge steel caskets and your second mahogany (or walnut) to relate to maple and oak caskets. The overriding consideration always is to maintain a *progression of value.*

One other factor needs to be taken into consideration before you finalize your price lines and your price points. The analysis presented here is based on the premise that the *material* used in the construction of a casket is the most important differentiating factor in demonstrating value progression to the consumer. Perhaps this is an arguable proposition. Perhaps the differences are reflected in the weight of metal (48-ounce versus 32-ounce), type of interior (velvet versus crepe), or shape of casket (round-cornered versus square-cornered). These are legitimate differences and they do enter into the equation of building a model stock assortment.

It is a question, however, of primary differences versus secondary differences. It is further a question of *comprehension* on the part of the consumer, given the consumer's overall lack of awareness about the nuances of casket features.

There is a problem in my view, when we try to put into our model stock caskets of one type of material that are more expensive than another—for example, copper caskets that are more expensive than bronze caskets; steel caskets that are more expensive than stainless steel caskets; cherry caskets that are more expensive than mahogany caskets, and so on. Clearly, because of legitimate wholesale cost differences, a 48-ounce urn-shaped copper casket might cost more to manufacture than a 32-ounce square-cornered bronze casket. At wholesale, therefore, it must be priced accordingly by the manufacturer. The problem comes in when you apply a conventional markup to this casket; you end up with a copper casket selling for more than some bronze caskets.

From the perspective of model stock planning, this should be avoided whenever possible. It is potentially confusing to the consumer. This is not to suggest that manufacturers refrain from offering types of caskets with overlapping wholesale prices. Keep in mind that suppliers must serve the broad needs of the industry. At this time, a very small number of funeral homes—*less than one percent of the industry*—are planning assortments in the context of a model stock program—with fully developed price lines and price points.

Further, keep in mind that the model stock plan needs to be tailored to the individual circumstances of each funeral home. A 48-ounce urn-shaped copper casket, for example, might very well be classified as "best" in some model stock assortments.

PRICE LISTS

Because of the 1984 FTC ruling, all funeral homes now have itemized price lists. The regulations, of course, require that funeral homes "unbundle" their services and products. Service charges must be itemized by major category. Merchandise must be clearly identified, itemized, and priced by individual item.

Not only is it required by law, it is good business to present to the consumer a clearcut and straightforward price list of the services and the products that you offer for sale. With regard to the casket merchandise aspect of the price list, Exhibit H is illustrative of a format that is clear cut and easy for the consumer to understand. This price list is easily printed on a 11" x 17" page, folded in the center. It is large enough to allow the listing of all metal caskets on one side of the page and all wood caskets on the other side.

Whether the metal is on the left and wood on the right, or vice versa, is not totally immaterial. If you are in a market where metal is preferred over wood, place that portion of the list to the right side, as this typically is the easiest side to read when dealing with a folded page. Note that the price list itself is *organized* first on the basis of material. Second, it is *classified* on the basis of the good–better–best principle, but these words do not appear on the list itself. The principle is made operational by virtue of the subcategories, such as bronze, copper, stainless steel, steel, mahogany/walnut, cherry, maple/oak, and pine/poplar/cloth covered or whatever is appropriate to the situation.

EXHIBIT H
EXAMPLE FUNERAL HOME CASKET PRICE LIST

WOOD CASKETS			
NAME	*FEATURE*	*INTERIOR*	*PRICE*
SOLID MAHOGANY, WALNUT			
Monarch	Parquetry	Velvet	$7,000
Presidential	Hand-rubbed	Velvet	4,500
Senator	Classic shape	Velvet	4,250
Chancellor	Dark finish	Velvet	4,250
SOLID CHERRY, MAPLE, OAK			
Congressional	Classic	Velvet	3,775
Cambridge	Post corners	Velvet	3,575
Regal	Natural	Velvet	3,375
Talisman	Colonial	Velvet	3,375
Marquis	Carved accents	Velvet	2,975
Ventura	Religious motifs	Crepe	2,775
PINE, POPLAR, COMPOSITION			
Liberty	Colonial	Crepe	2,295
Meridian	Understated	Crepe	2,095
Dominion	Dark finish	Crepe	1,895
Oakland	Lacquer	Crepe	1,695
Columbus	Veneer	Crepe	1,295
Dunlop	Composition	Crepe	795

METALCASKETS			
NAME	*FEATURE*	*INTERIOR*	*PRICE*
SOLID BRONZE			
Ambassador	Brushed	Ultrasuede	$7,000
Imperial	Brushed	Velvet	5,500
Winston	Brushed	Velvet	4,750
Franklin	Brushed	Velvet	4,450
SOLID COPPER, STAINLESS			
Diplomat	Brushed	Velvet	3,775
Commander	Brushed	Velvet	3,575
Statesman	Brushed	Velvet	3,375
Remington	Brushed	Velvet	3,375
Electra	Brushed	Velvet	2,975
Royale	Brushed	Velvet	2,775
STEEL			
Bel Air	Painted	Velvet	2,495
Sonata	Painted	Velvet	2,295
Requiem	Painted	Crepe	2,095
Celeste	Painted	Crepe	1,895
Harmony	Painted	Crepe	1,495
Avalon	Painted	Crepe	995

If you are in a market where metal sales are considerably stronger than wood sales, or vice versa, you may not want to have one whole page for metal and another page for wood. You may want to use a page presentation that gives less emphasis to one material over the other. This is quite all right. It is a format used by Batesville with its "Value Approach." Its limitation is that it does not feature the good–better–best principle as dramatically, nor does it have as clearcut a presentation of value progression for wood caskets.

In view of the fact that this is a *consumer price list*, it does not refer at all to manufacturer name or number. These have been replaced with consumer-oriented names as discussed in Chapter 2. The price list exhibited includes a brief description of the most unique feature of each product in the assortment. This adds dimension to the price list and makes it more helpful to the consumer.

PRICE SIGNS

An integral part of good pricing is the development of a straightforward sign program that communicates with the customer—first by providing useful information about the product, and second, by clearly showing the price. Certainly, we can do better than the typed/printed cards that are placed in the bed of the casket or the metal signs with price only placed on the closed foot of the casket.

Signing is important because we have a responsibility to inform our customers about the features and benefits of the products that are in our assortment. This is doubly important in funeral service since customers know *so very little* about what they are looking at to begin with.

I recommend a sign program that is in keeping with what would be found in a high level specialty store. As illustrated in Exhibit I, such a sign is attractively framed and mounted on the wall behind the casket—over the closed lid portion of the casket. On full-couch caskets, a special bracket is used to hold the sign.

The sign itself identifies the name of the casket, e.g., "The President," and highlights the features and benefits of the casket, and then shows the price in numerals that are large enough in size to be plainly visible from a distance of three to four feet.

Feedback from funeral home owners and managers who have used this type of signing has been overwhelmingly positive. Consumers volunteer that they *appreciate* the size and straightforward character of the signs, especially the clear way that prices are presented.

Funeral arrangers appreciate these signs also. They make it easier to serve consumers because less information needs to be communicated verbally.

EXHIBIT I
CASKET SIGNING WITH A CONSUMER FOCUS

THE PRESIDENT

• Solid Mahogany
• Eight-sided Mitered Corners
• Hand-rubbed Finish
• Tailored Velvet Interior

$4,500

PRICE POLICY

Fortunately for funeral service, pricing is rarely blatant or intense. There is considerable latitude in pricing funeral services and products. *This is as it should be.*

Funeral service is not a monolithic service and product offer! It is a creative and high value-added business. It is, in a sense, like a fine hotel or restaurant; it is partially an art form. Substantial differences exist between the offers of different companies—in location of facilities, in quality of facilities, in intrinsic services provided, in attitude and competence of personnel, in assortments of funeral-related products offered for sale, in advertising and promotion effectiveness, in pre-need sales success, and in prices charged.

This book is about making these differences greater than they are now—encouraging the progressive firm to *distance itself* from its competition—just as Ritz Carlton has done from Hilton and Wal-Mart has done from Kmart. Note, however, that the quest for competitive advantage is not taking an "up-scale" approach, per se, as in the case of Ritz Carlton. The quest is to be superior in what *you* do—so that you control your own destiny. This means carving a niche in the marketplace that *insulates* you from low profit or profit-less competition.

CHAPTER 4

REINVENTING YOUR SELECTION ROOM ENVIRONMENT

Good design is the basis for good communication.

—Stephen A. Klimont, AIA
Creative Communications for a Successful Design Practice

Suppose that you are planning to build a new funeral home and that it is to be state of the art in every aspect.

What will your casket selection room look like? What will your other product displays look like and where will they be located? Will they be *in* the casket selection room, in the arrangement offices, or in some other location in the facility?

How big should the casket selection room be? How many caskets should it hold? What should the general room configuration be? What about special fixtures and displays, and what about lighting, color schemes, and carpeting?

These are legitimate questions. It is the purpose of this chapter and the next chapter to answer these questions—not only for planning new funeral homes, but more importantly, for the reformatting of existing funeral homes.

PROTOTYPE PLANNING

In my former company, Retail Planning Associates, I had the opportunity to design stores for successful retailers around the world. Because of the complexity of retailing—where thousands or even hundreds of thousands of SKU's are handled—retailers are continually developing "state of the art" prototype stores or prototype departments within stores. Such prototypes are invaluable in the building of new facilities, the expansion of existing facilities and in the remodeling of existing facilities. It may not be possible to bring older facilities to the same level of perfection as the new ones, but they can be changed significantly to improve productivity and profitability. The purpose of the prototype then, is to establish the planning *benchmarks.*

Funeral Products from Different Perspectives

Knowing what you know about making funeral arrangements, you are aware that for the ultimate consumer entering the selection room is the most difficult part of the entire funeral arrangement process. Solid research shows that consumers are very apprehensive and know almost nothing about what to expect.[13] There is the experience of initial shock, and the bewilderment of having to choose, rather quickly, from product lines that they know very little about and don't *want* to know very much about.

There is also the problem of the arranger, who at present is the principal conduit of information regarding funeral-related products. Owners and managers sometimes question the attitudes and the performance of arrangers, especially those who consistently write business below the

[13]Paul E. Irion. *The Funeral: Vestige or Value?* (Nashville, Tennessee: Parthenon Press, 1966), pp. 67-69.

funeral home's required average sale. While this is a legitimate concern, perhaps the solution has been incorrectly identified in the past. The conventional wisdom would prescribe more effective "product" or "sales" training. Perhaps that's not the answer. Maybe the buying process for caskets and other funeral-related products is just so unique that it is beyond the capacity of anyone to explain it thoroughly.

Remember the axiom of avoiding "doing better things that we should not be doing at all." Arranger training is not *the* fundamental solution to assisting customers in making more intelligent buying decisions. It is creative *model stock planning*—the subject of Chapter 2, straightforward pricing—the subject of Chapter 3, and *good selection room planning and design*—the subject of this chapter.

THE SELECTION ROOM

Let your imagination run freely and think about an ideal selection room from a *consumer* point of view. Disregard, for the moment, traditional restraints involving number of caskets, size of room, and cost of room.

This is not as outlandish as you may think because the *incremental* cost of building the ideal or state of the art selection room—over and above what you would spend anyway—is not very great when it is considered in the total scheme of things. We will analyze costs and return on investment in detail in the next chapter.

Exhibit J on the following page depicts a "state of the art" selection room. Examine the layout carefully and note that is *not* a single room, but a small and large room linked together.

The Explanation Room

The small room, or anteroom, is a new type of explanation grouping containing six caskets—three on each side of the space. On one side are three metal caskets—good, better, best—and on the other side—three wood caskets—good, better, and best.

If we think back to our "typical funeral home" serving a broad market, the principle might be interpreted as steel–copper–bronze and pine–maple–mahogany. But, as previously noted, it might be otherwise, depending upon the specific objectives of the model stock plan and the specific market to be served. There are important features about this explanation room.

First, since it is small and intimate, it is less shocking and intimidating to the consumer than a full-scale casket selection room.

Second, since there are three wood caskets and three metal caskets, it immediately lets the consumer know about the two *basic types* of caskets from which a choice can be made.

Third, the consumer immediately can see and understand the concept of *good, better, best* because the specific choice of caskets in the explanation grouping has been carefully planned to show *value differences* in the progression from good to better to best.

In identifying the specific caskets for the explanation grouping, it is essential that there be a *sharp differentiation* from one casket to another. In choosing the specific items, the general rule would be that the steel casket would always be a painted casket. It is never brushed and probably not even shaded. However, it is not a low-end defensive unit. It

EXHIBIT J
A STATE OF THE ART SELECTION ROOM

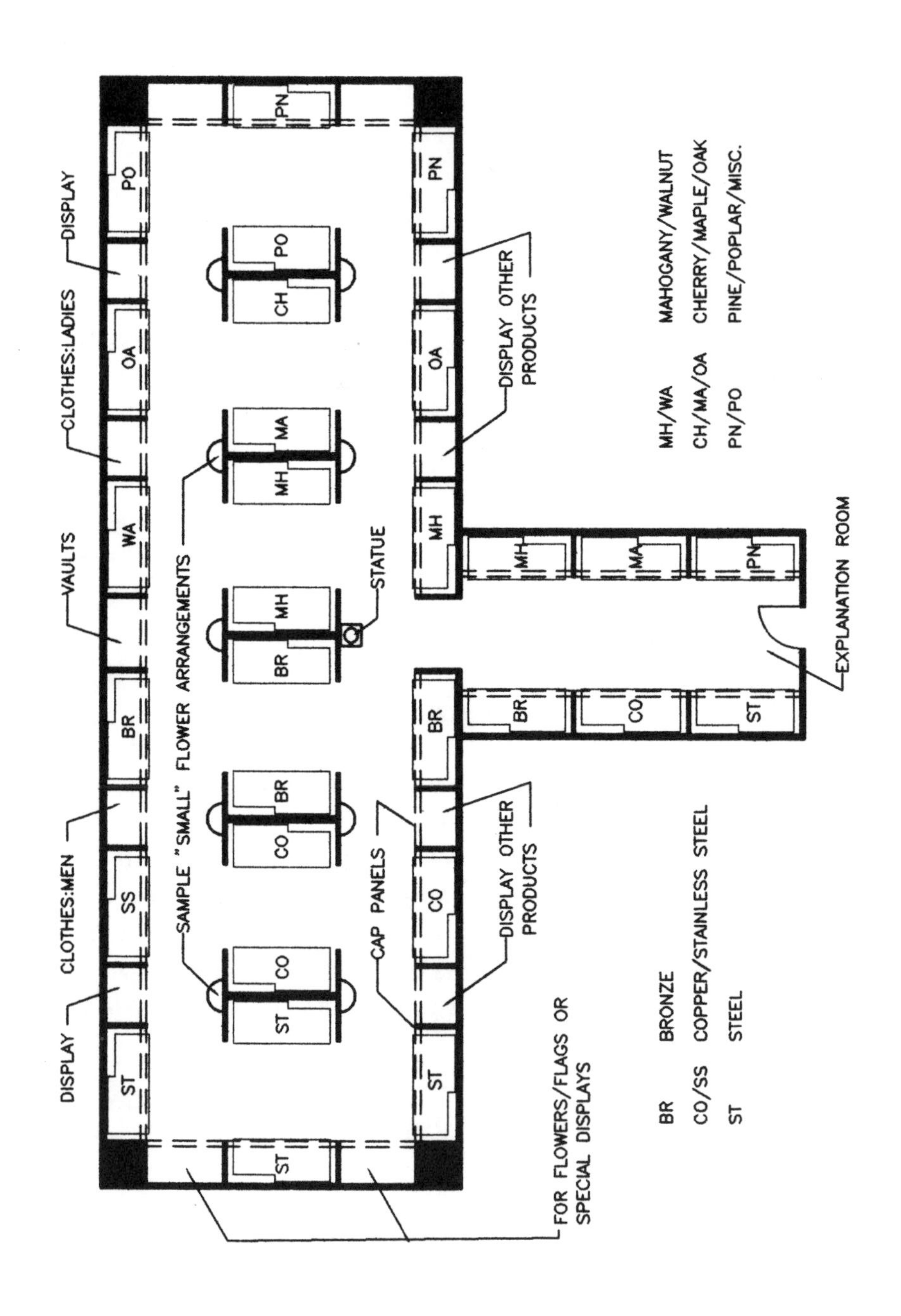

is more likely to be an attractive 18-gauge casket with a crepe interior representing a mid-priced steel casket. The copper casket (or stainless) is always shown with a brushed finish and a velvet interior. The brushed finish allows thecon-sumer is to grasp quickly that copper is a non-rusting, semi-precious metal or that stainless is superior to the regular metal. The bronze casket is shown with a brushed and shaded finish, with a velvet interior and fine hardware that makes it stand out from the copper or the stainless casket.

Likewise, the pine casket, with a crepe interior, is selected to typify the wood caskets in the "good" classification. The maple casket is shown as a "better" product, with a much finer finish and with a velvet interior. The mahogany casket is selected to reflect truly fine furniture, with perhaps more of a hand-rubbed finish and velvet interior.

The casket shells and the interiors in the explanation grouping are color-coordinated. This allows each unit to stand out, one from the other, and show a representative sample of the color variations that are available to the consumer. Caskets and interiors also must feature different shell shapes and interior designs.

Suppose that we are planning this room for a somewhat typical, broad market. We might choose a medium-to-dark blue exterior and a light blue interior (with shirring) for the 18-gauge steel casket. We might choose a mid-color lavender exterior with a pink interior (somewhat tailored) for the copper casket. For the bronze casket, we might select a dark gray exterior with a white interior (fully tailored). The shell shapes might feature a rounded-corner for the steel, a square corner with decorated ends for the copper, and an urn-shaped for the bronze.

For wood caskets, we might choose for the pine a medium brown stain, with a white crepe interior; for the maple, a natural stain with a dark or medium green velvet interior, and for the mahogany a medium red stain, with an ecru interior. As a general rule, the interiors should range from "busy" in appearance on the low end to finely "tailored" on the high end. There could be exceptions to this, of course, depending upon the actual customer profile of the funeral home.

Oftentimes, there are questions about such things as a "green" interior for the maple casket. We know that this is not going be to a big seller. It is not intended to be. But keep in mind that this is your explanation grouping—your "sample" room. It is somewhat analogous to a dramatic display in a department store. You may not buy the yellow sport coat that you see on the mannikin, but it gets your attention! That's its purpose—to stimulate your thinking about buying *a* new sport coat. It's OK with the store if you end up buying a blue blazer.

The explanation room in this configuration is 360 square feet. Study it carefully. This room may well be the most important square footage in your entire facility. It provides an unparalleled opportunity to *serve your customer*, to teach and advise about a unique product that is purchased infrequently and for which the consumer has little or no knowledge. The explanation room provides unparalleled *support* for your arrangers, who can now for the first time, effectively communicate a complex message to the consumer in a short period of time because you have given them the tools to do the job.

The Main Selection Room

If you refer to the floor plan shown in Exhibit J, you will see that the main selection room is organized to feature metal caskets on one side of the room and wood caskets on the other. There are a total of six worlds—with four separate "niches" for caskets in each. Each niche can hold a single casket or—with newly designed double racks—can hold two caskets—one above the other. The significance of the new racks, compared with those that have been used in the industry for years, is that they are unobtrusive. In fact, they cannot be seen *at all* when caskets are placed on them. Further, the frame holding the top casket is only 27 inches from the floor, which means that the top casket is not much higher than it would be if it were placed on a conventional bier.

The total capacity of the main room (not including the explanation room) is 24 caskets if they are displayed as singles and 48 caskets if they are displayed as doubles. In actuality, some units no doubt would be displayed as singles and others as doubles. The "ideal" mix might be a room with a 42 to 46 unit configuration.

Traffic Circulation and Layout

It is the *traffic circulation plan* and the *layout* of this state of the art selection room that makes it possible for the stock to be *organized* so that one side of the room is devoted entirely to metal and the other side is devoted entirely to wood. It is the *layout* that makes it possible for the stock to be further *classified* into good, better, and best—with a specific bronze world, copper/stainless world, steel world, a mahogany/walnut world, cherry/maple/oak world and a pine/poplar/cloth-covered world or whatever else is appropriate. It is the *layout* that permits maximum impact and exposure such that the units within each world *face each other*. Once the consumer is inside of a particular world, he or she can turn 360 degrees and see the entire assortment in that world. This is a unique feature of this layout. Each world has the capacity for four to eight units, depending upon whether a double or single casket configuration is shown.

Vistas and Focal Points

There are other special features of this state of the art room. Upon entering the main room—after finishing with the explanation, there is a small bronze statue on a pedestal. The purpose of this is to *block the line of sight* from the explanation room into the main selection room. The statue becomes a "focal point" to soften the room and set the tone upon entering the room.

Turning either to the right or left and looking to the very end of the room, there are niches with flower arrangements in them. There are also brackets on the end walls dividing the worlds which can hold smaller flower arrangements. These flower arrangements help set the tone for the room—reducing harshness and severity. They are designed so that the customer's "line of sight" sees something other than caskets when looking down to the end of the room.

While some funeral homes might use these flower arrangements for strictly decorative purposes, ideally they should be representative of flower arrangements that families could purchase in connection with a funeral. This is really quite practical now that silk flowers can be made to look almost exactly like real ones. In some markets, of course, the silk flowers could be made available on a rental basis.

Other Funeral Products

On the side walls dividing the worlds, in between the large casket niches, are smaller niches for the display of other funeral-related products. Alternatively, these niches can serve as closets with doors on them. In this case, they might hold clothing or other funeral-related products that are not kept on open display. The doors of the closets have special concealed architectural hinges and handles, so that the flat surfaces can serve as background for the display of cap panels. Each door holds three cap panels for a total of 12 on the metal side of the room and 12 on the wood side of the room.

Altogether, 24 cap panel positions could be shown in the room. It may be, however, that identical cap panels are shown on the wood side of the room and the metal side of the room. It is important to avoid confusion over secondary features such as cap panels. It is not a good idea, for example, to have the funeral arranger or the consumer move back and forth from the wood to metal sections of the room, unless, of course, the consumer desires to do this.

In the very center of the selection room, on the rear wall, there is a special niche to hold the vault display *between* the metal and the wood sections of the room. This is a built-in display, designed for scale-model vaults. It can feature in a dramatic way, the entire line of the manufacturer. It can be an open display or it can be behind closed doors depending on the point of view of the funeral home owner or manager.

If metal vaults are to be featured, this could be done in the same niche by the use of pictures. If composite and metal vaults are to be sold, the metal vaults could be pictured on the wing wall opposite the vault niche. If this were to be done, this wing wall should have a recess built into it so that the pictures are not just “hanging” on the wall.

It is my personal preference to have the vault display behind closed doors so that the consumer can concentrate on the casket purchase *before* considering the vault purchase. There are two reasons for this. First, as noted above, the casket-purchasing process can be confusing in and of itself. Second, a vault oftentimes is chosen to go with a casket. It follows, therefore, that the vault decision should be made after the casket decision. If the vault display is behind closed doors, the doors must swing 180 degrees on their hinges so that they are completely out of the way at the time the consumer is in front of the vault display.

Overall Size and Capacity

The overall size of the main selection room in this ideal prototype—as shown on Exhibit J—is 2,140 square feet in size. The total size of the room—explanation grouping and main room—is 2,400 square feet. While the size of this room is somewhat larger than most selection rooms being built today, it is not necessarily *too* large. A cardinal rule in architecture and design is that *form follows function.* If such a room really improves customer service, arranger effectiveness and company profitability, it can be justified in terms of return on investment. This subject is taken up in detail in Chapter 5, which follows.

In addressing the question of size and function, keep in mind that this prototype has been developed from the *consumer's* point of view. When this is done, the relevant number is *not* the total number of caskets in the room. It is "6" to begin with—the number shown in the explanation room. Then, based upon customer preference, the relevant number is not the "24" to "48" unit total capacity of the main room, but the "4," "6," or "8"—the number of caskets on display in the *world* that the customer is considering at the moment.

Fixtures, Display and Merchandise Presentation

There is an old adage in retailing—the *merchandise itself is the presentation.*

Accordingly, caskets should be presented on biers, pedestals, or double racks that do not visually interfere with the image of the product itself. This would rule out ornamental biers of all types as these detract from the merchandise. Also, many of those that are in use today are downright old-fashioned in appearance, gaudy, beat up and ugly. In recent years, manufacturers have provided their customers, at nominal cost, with acrylic hexagonal pedestals which are simple and attractive. They are unobtrusive and colorless. Some funeral directors object to them on the grounds that they make caskets appear to be "levitating," but I personally think that they are a practical and flexible solution.

The ideal casket display fixture is a rectangular or oval-shaped upholstered pedestal. It can be padded, covered, and piped with material on the edges to have a tailored look. The fabric can be easily color-coordinated with the carpet. The cost of solid, good-looking pedestals is more than the acrylic pedestals, but they can be justified in funeral service. They enhance the quality of the casket and the appearance selection room.

Because of the shortage of space in the typical selection room, double racks for caskets have been used in the industry for years. Not finding a double rack on the market that I felt to be satisfactory from a merchandise presentation viewpoint, I assisted Batesville in developing a new rack for use in connection with the company's advanced merchandising Partnership Marketing Program. This rack has the advantage of being unobtrusive. It virtually disappears when two caskets are in position on it. In addition, it is low to the ground so that the top casket can be viewed easily when the lid is open.

Double racks serve a very important purpose *in addition to* adding to capacity. They make it possible for the funeral home to "make a statement" with featured caskets or categories of caskets. For example, a very popular unit can be shown in two different colors, with two interior colors. Wood caskets look particularly good when the same specie is shown one over the other.

DESIGN, DECOR AND LIGHTING

The disciplines of design, decor and lighting of selection rooms have not been among the strong points in funeral home planning up until this time. In fact, my friends and clients in funeral service, who have a good sense of humor, like to show "before and after" slides of their selection rooms—prior to their reconfiguration. The contrast is quite startling.

Good design is not "decorating." It is the development of the *overall physical plan that coordinates all of the tangible elements to achieve the desired results*. It is sensitive to the buying needs of the consumer and the merchandising needs of business.

At the heart of good design is proper space allocation, traffic circulation and layout. If these are not done correctly, no amount of money spent on "ambiance" is of much value. But the physical characteristics of the room are important—colors, patterns, textures, materials for ceilings, walls, partitions, and floors. They need to be coordinated with a lighting plan which features "task" lighting rather than overall "ambient" lighting. And, as noted earlier, there is the need or signing to assist the consumer in understanding the features of the specific products under consideration.

Remembering the adage, "the merchandise is the presentation," the challenge is to create a total ambiance, a mood, a feeling that is compatible with casket merchandise and other merchandise—given all of the different colors and physical characteristics of the products.

Color

In the opinion of experts, the colors blue and green do not work well for selection rooms. They look good with some products, but poor with others. Further, the color blue tends to project a "cold" feeling rather than a warm feeling.

Beige and gray (taupe gray, not blue gray) are fairly good choices as they are more neutral and they are more compatible with a broad range of product.

The ideal color palette consists of various hues of salmon, melon, and peach. When combined with proper lighting and carpeting, selection rooms done in these colors provide a remarkable background for casket merchandise—finished in just about any color of metal or any stain of wood. Flowers are also beautifully set off by colors in this palette.

Finishes, Textures and Carpets

Wall finishes can be enhanced if they have subtle textures. This can be achieved from variegated paint coatings or from wallpapers, where today there is an almost unlimited range of product from which to choose. Carpets should be subtle, devoid of too much pattern or texture. The specifications should be commensurate with the traffic that is anticipated. It is highly desirable to specify a commercial grade carpet with bonded padding permanently attached to it. This eliminates the headache of having to continually restretch the carpet because you are rolling heavy objects over it. Commercial-grade carpet with bonded padding is even more important if you are going to utilize double racks that create extra wear or markings on the surface of the carpet.

Ceilings and Lighting

Ceilings, in a modern selection room, should be of a "lay in" panel suspension type. They are relatively inexpensive and they are easy to modify when necessary. Also, they provide easy access to electrical and other mechanical systems that may require service from time to time. The newer versions of suspension ceilings are quite attractive. There is no longer the need to install a plain 2-by-4-foot grid with a smooth surface tile. A 2-by-2 grid with a patterned tile is far richer in appearance and the incremental cost is nominal.

Lighting, properly planned and installed, can greatly enhance the total merchandise presentation of the selection room. The general rule is to minimize the use of fluorescent fixtures, especially those that do not have parabolic lens covers to deflect the glare and the directness of the light. If a lay-in ceiling is used, recessed cone light fixtures are very practical. They can be equipped with directional lenses, so that the light can be focused exactly where it should be. However, track lighting also can be used. It is less expensive than the recessed cone fixtures and it is far and away the most flexible lighting system available. Further, if you are using soffits as part of the design of your selection room, track lighting is ideal, as it can be installed on the back side of the soffit partitions in a way that is not visible to the consumer.

Smaller Prototypes

Having developed an ideal "state of the art" prototype, incorporating all of the characteristics that we would want under the best of circumstances, it is now possible to make practical adjustments that may be required for one reason or another.

It might be that the land available for the new building is simply too tight to allocate the square footage suggested above. It might be that we are planning a relatively small funeral home—and that we cannot justify the incremental investment in space or in inventory. It might be that we are in a high-cost metropolitan area, where land and building costs are double average costs, requiring the rethinking of all conventional planning premises about funeral homes.

These are real and practical restraints. They require modifications to the ideal prototype. Exhibit K is illustrative of such a modification. This plan is approximately 27% (750 square feet) smaller than the ideal prototype for a total of 1,750 square feet. This prototype accommodates up to 42 caskets *without compromising many of the essential concepts* of the larger plan. The explanation grouping is identical to the prototype and the division between metal and wood is maintained. The worlds remain in place. However, they are not defined quite as precisely as they are in the previous plan. The "best" world is now confined to the two middle niches in the first section. The "better" world is adjacent to the "best" world and the "good" world is next to it. In this prototype, one or more of the niches could be regarded as a swing area, which means that it could be used for better merchandise or for good merchandise.

Note that most of the important aspects of the ideal plan are preserved. The vista with the statue at the entrance to the room is maintained. Four (instead of eight) of the smaller niches or closets are maintained, permitting the display of flowers or the storage of clothing and the display of cap panels, but fewer than before. The special niche for vaults remains exactly as it is in the ideal prototype.

Exhibit L is an even smaller derivative of the prototype—approximately 40% smaller than the ideal prototype. It is 1,425 total square feet in size, with a capacity for up to

EXHIBIT K
A STATE OF THE ART SELECTION ROOM
DOWNSIZED VERSION

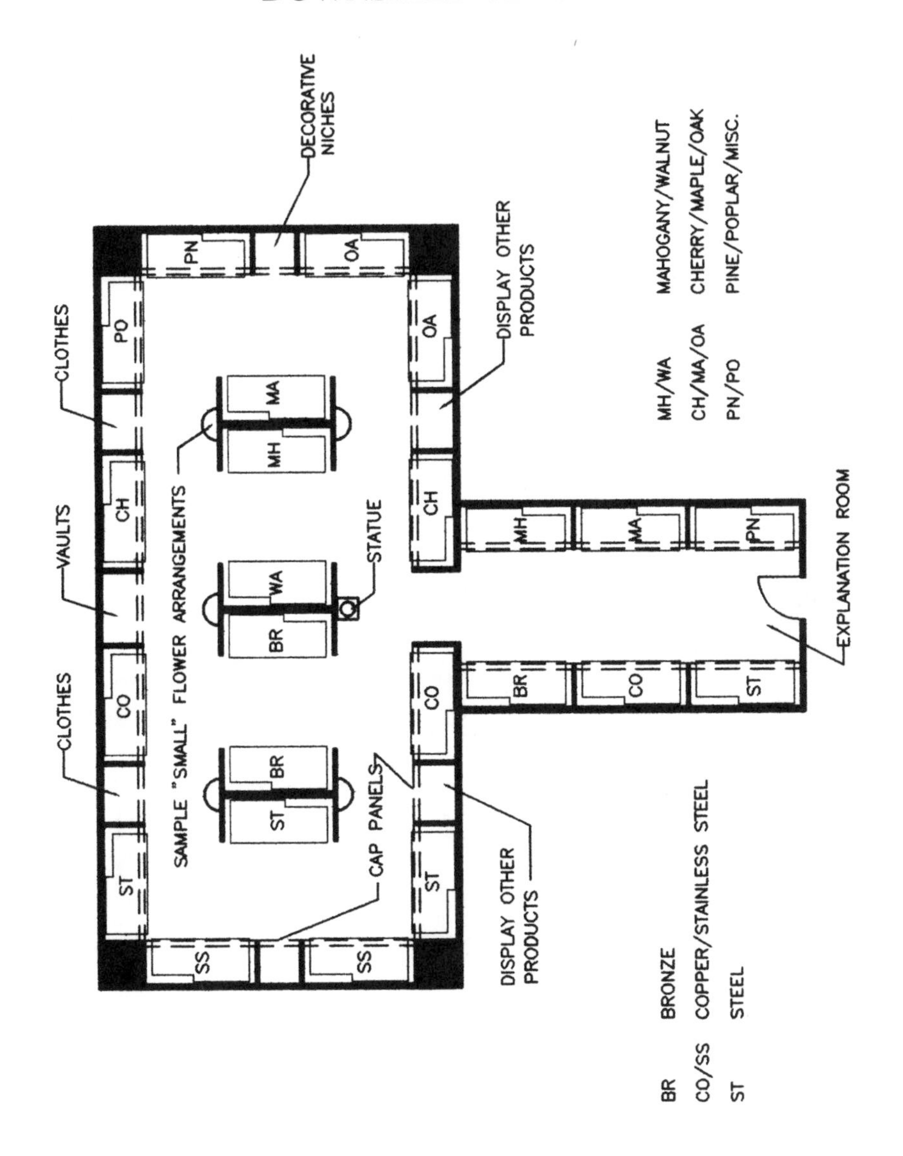

34 caskets. This prototype configuration could be used in markets where the model stock is decidedly metal rather than wood or vice versa as one side of the main room is now reduced to a single section with five niches, for a maximum presentation capacity of 10 caskets.

EXHIBIT L
A STATE OF THE ART SELECTION ROOM
SMALLER VERSION

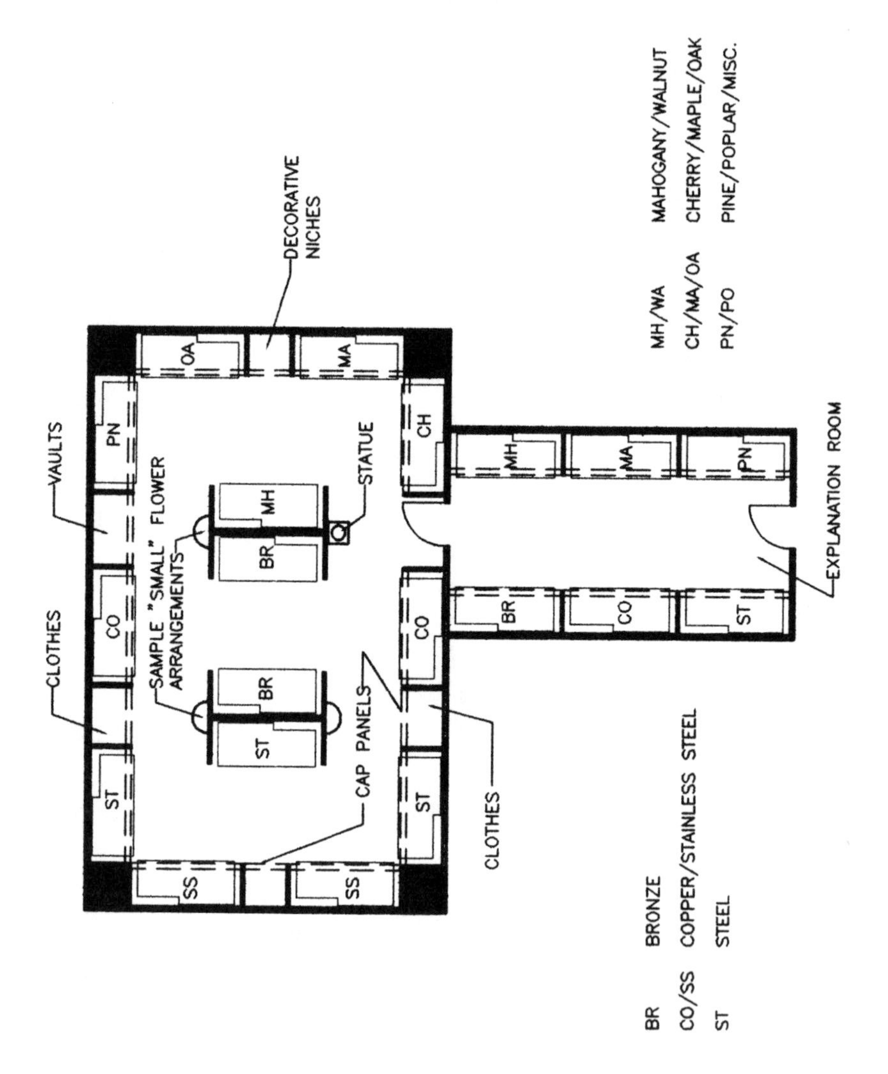

Prototype Derivatives

As mentioned in the beginning of this chapter, the purpose of a prototype is to set specific parameters for the planning and design of new selection rooms and to positively influence the retrofitting of existing rooms. The basic features that have been designed into the prototypes are:

1. A separate explanation room.
2. A carefully delineated assortment for the explanation room.
3. A large main selection room with sufficient capacity to provide the consumer with a wide choice.
4. A sharply defined main casket selection room organized with separate metal and wood areas.
5. A fully developed classification system creating "worlds" for good–better–best.
6. Separate niches to more effectively set off one casket from another.
7. The use of double racks to practically accommodate large assortments.
8. The careful consideration of "sight lines" and "vistas."
9. The use of auxiliary decorative elements, such as statues.
10. The incorporation of special displays for other funeral-related merchandise, including flowers, clothing, cap panels and vaults.
11. The careful coordination of all design elements—including color, texture, carpet and lighting.
12. The use of category signs and item signs to help the consumer identify products by type and personal preference.

Prototype derivatives strive to incorporate as many features as possible from the main prototypes—given the practical constraints of existing conditions.

Exhibit M is an illustration of such a derivative. It is a plan developed for maximum efficiency. It has been used by a number of existing funeral homes it is readily adaptable to existing space. This room has a capacity to house up to 28 caskets in 975 square feet.

While it does not have a separate explanation room, the layout of the room lends itself to easy explanation owing to the fact that the customer can immediately see wood caskets on one side of the room and metal caskets on the other. In fact, from a position in the center of the room, the arranger can point out all of the different types of caskets as they are visible from this perspective.

Exhibit N is a larger prototype derivative—developed for the new Caruth-Hale Funeral Home in Hot Springs, Arkansas. It is 1,290 square feet in size and has a capacity of 36 caskets. It has the advantage of more clearly defined worlds than what is possible with the smaller room.

Exhibit O is a larger prototype derivative—developed initially for the All Faiths Funeral Home in New Orleans, Louisiana. This selection room is 1,460 square feet in size and has the capacity to house up to 46 units. However, at this time, the owner has elected to display 41 units in a configuration of 18 double units and 5 single units, which are planned as focal points.

Note that the clothes closet is not in this selection room, but immediately adjacent to it. One of the arrangement offices has a large closet with bifold doors, specifically designed to display children's caskets.

EXHIBITS M AND N
PROTOTYPE DERIVATIVE SELECTION ROOMS

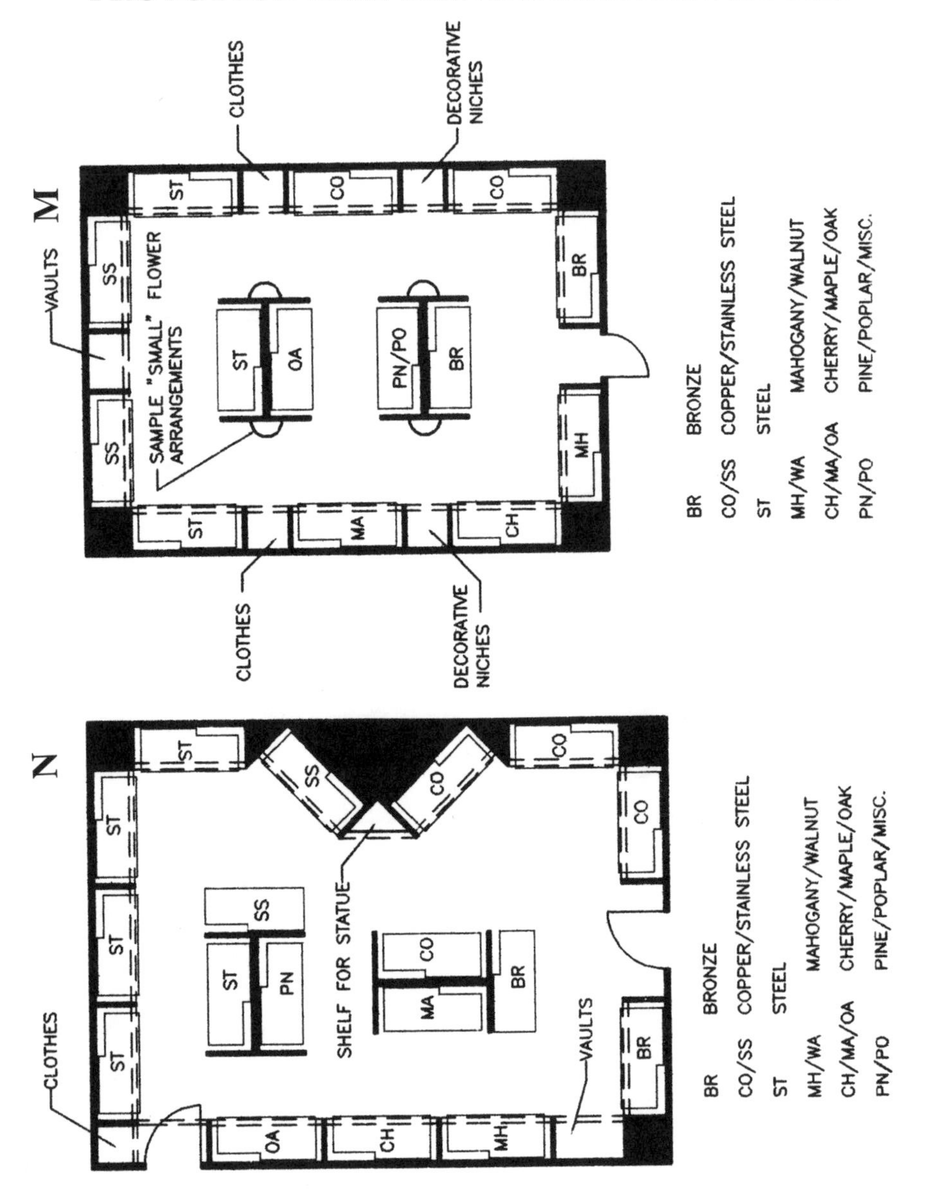

EXHIBIT O
PROTOTYPE DERIVATIVE SELECTION ROOM WITH ADJACENT ARRANGEMENT OFFICES

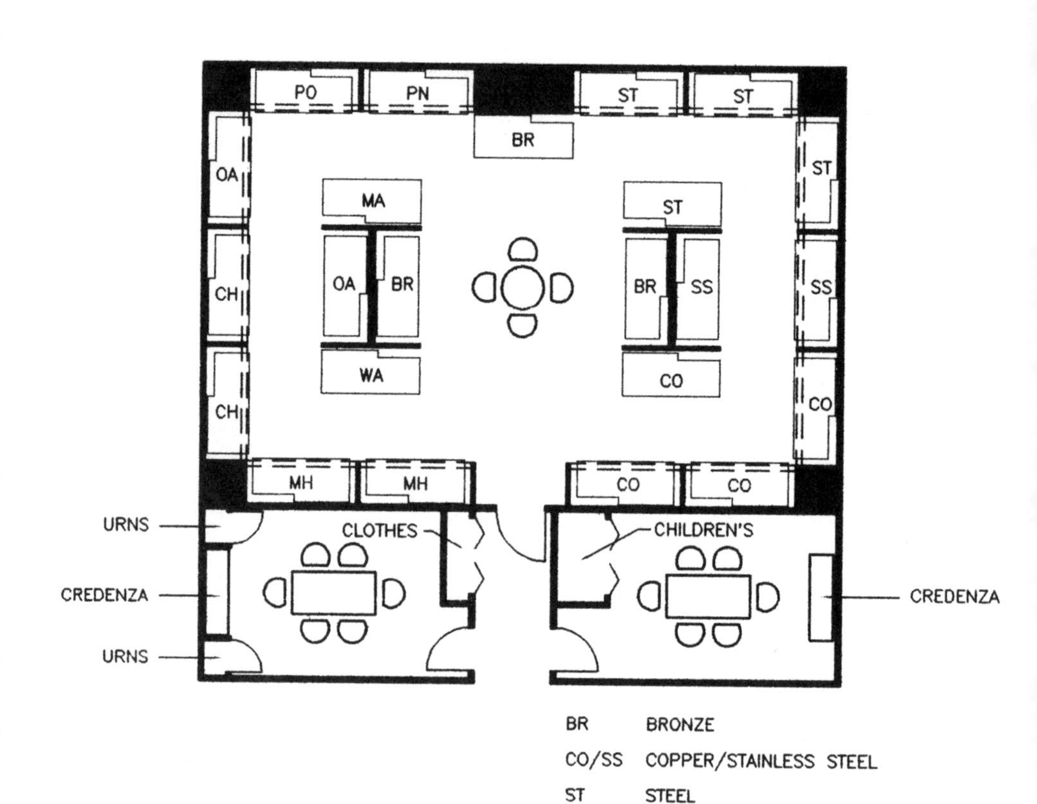

BR BRONZE
CO/SS COPPER/STAINLESS STEEL
ST STEEL
MH/WA MAHOGANY/WALNUT
CH/MA/OA CHERRY/MAPLE/OAK
PN/PO PINE/POPLAR/MISC.

Incorporated into the arrangement offices are built-in bookcase fixtures for the display of urns. These are fitted with glass shelves and conical down lights to enhance the merchandise presentation.

Note that the arrangement offices are furnished with a conference table, a credenza and six chairs. This configuration has proved to be vastly superior to the old style setup, where the arranger sat behind a desk. Conference-style seating allows for better eye-to-eye contact and a more relaxed setting generally.

The Merchandising of Monuments, Markers and Other Funeral-related Products

The principles of assortment planning, pricing and merchandise presentation and display are the same for all other lines of funeral-related products.

Generally speaking, funeral homes do a pitifully poor job of merchandising these lines. Assortments are limited and display fixtures are sometimes nothing more than the floor for monuments, a bare wall for markers, and a table with a book for everything else.

Exhibit P shows a new concept for the merchandising of monuments and markers developed by The Doody Group for the Pine Crest Funeral Home in Mobile, Alabama in conjunction with the Matthews Bronze Division of Matthews International. Adjacent to the business entrance, which is used for arrangements and cemetery inquiries, is a special outdoor display area for monuments and markers. The space is 1,540 square feet in size. It will accommodate a product assortment consisting of 28 monuments, plus markers, and a number of different cemetery and mausoleum flower vases. The area is covered with a vinyl mesh, umbrella-like fabric to reduce glare and heat. There are category signs, price signs and special lighting.

EXHIBIT P
PROTOTYPE OUTDOOR SELECTION AREA FOR MONUMENTS AND MARKERS

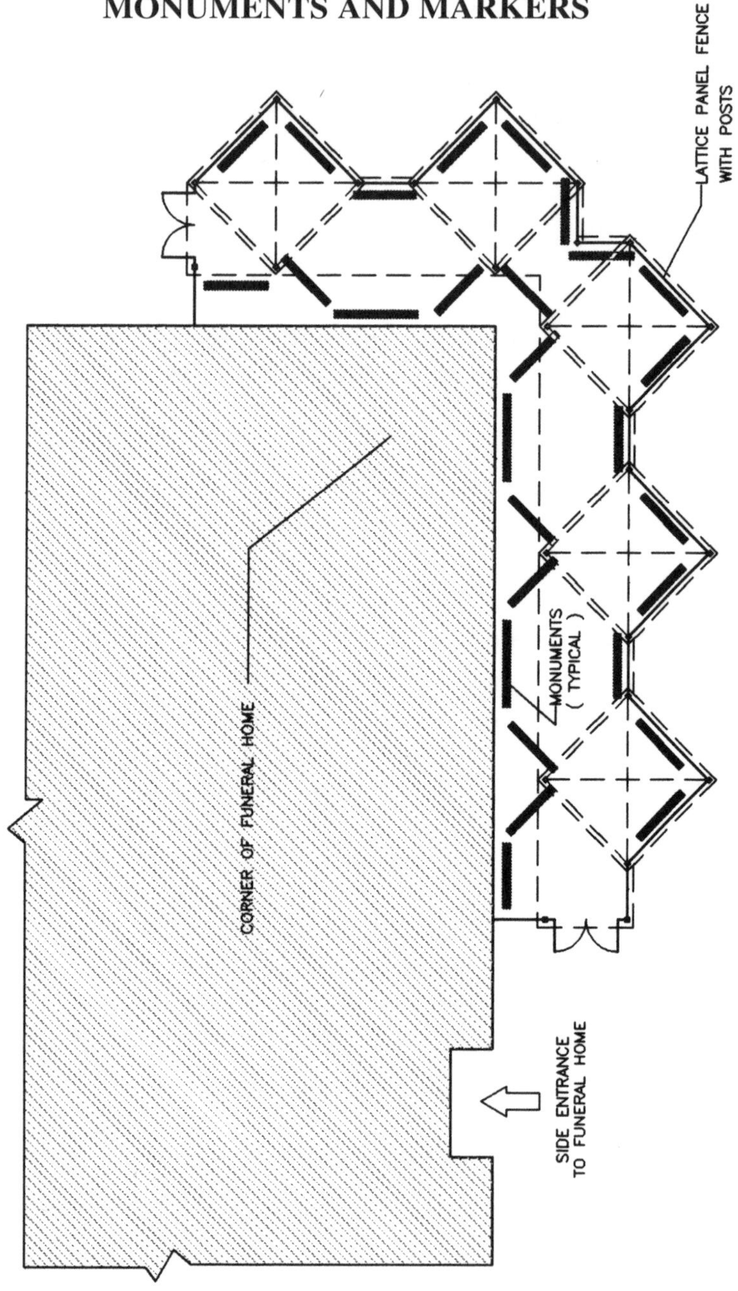

SUMMARY

Professionally developed model stock assortments, pricing policies and funeral product environments are not ends in themselves. They are means toward ends.

The ends are more satisfied customers, more effective arranger personnel and greater cash flow and profits for the firm. It is now time to consider the financial costs and returns that are associated with advanced merchandising programs. This is the subject of Chapter 5 to follow. As stated at the outset of this book, the costs are modest and the risks are low. The returns are substantial.

CHAPTER 5

REINVENTING YOUR PROFIT OPPORTUNITY

Never have so many owed so much to so few . . . .

—Winston Spencer Churchill
The Battle of Britain, 1940

There are risks and costs to a program of action, but they are far less than the long-range risks and costs of comfortable inaction.

—John F. Kennedy

Let's suppose that our "typical funeral home" serving a broad market embarked upon a systematic program to build a model stock program for *all* funeral-related product categories—those bought for resale and those handled on an agency basis. Let's further suppose that this funeral home rationalized its pricing structure with price lines and price points showing a step-by-step progression of value from good, to better, to best. Let's also suppose that this funeral home created a professional environment for the sale of these products—inside the selection room for some lines of products and outside for others—but in every case assorted, displayed, priced, signed, and lighted in a way that made it easy for the customer to make decisions.

What kind of increase in sales could be achieved? What kind of increase in cash flow and profit could be achieved? The truth is that *no one* really knows at this time! The reason that no one knows is that no funeral home has yet *implemented a total program to put all of the elements together.*

Programmed Merchandising: Recent Developments

Within the last several years, considerable progress has been made on the casket element of merchandising; quite a lot of progress has been made with cremation products, and some progress with vaults. And, as mentioned in the preceding chapter, a pioneering project is underway to develop a total merchandising program for monuments, markers and related products.

But the opportunity for the industry is altogether in the future! Even casket merchandising programs are in their infancy. At the time of this writing—in the summer of 1993—there are only a hundred or so really advanced programs up and running. There are several hundred additional "large assortment" installations based on the principles espoused in Chapter 2. And, no doubt, there are several hundred other reasonably well-developed assortments in place throughout the country. Nevertheless, relative to the potential, the surface barely has been scratched!

We know this empirically, based on the results of the partial programs that are in place. A fully developed casket merchandising program alone can easily achieve a $200, $300 or $400 average sales increase. And, many, many programs achieve results considerably higher than this. A well-planned cremation products program can achieve a $100 to $200 average increase, as can a well-merchandised vault program. The embryonic programs that are in place for other lines of funeral products are so new that little data are available at this time. However, everything suggests that additional sales increases are possible from these lines of products also.

What then is the cumulative sales impact of a total merchandising program—as described herein—on a funeral home? In the final analysis, you will have to use your own judgment to determine just what your firm can achieve. In doing so, however, don't be too conservative!

Remember that we are talking about a straightforward approach that has been proven successful in other lines of business. Remember too that this approach really does serve customers by making available to them, on a one-stop shopping basis, large assortments of products that are needed by them. Remember also, that the approach serves arrangers better by actually making their job more achievable.

Incremental Sales

Exhibit Q, shown on the following page, is a table developed in matrix form to show the total sales potential of such a program based upon different volume assumptions. The number of calls is shown on the vertical axis and the average dollar sales increase is shown on the horizontal axis.

An examination of this table reveals that impressive sales improvements are possible. Even a one-hundred call firm that achieves a $200 average sales increase will augment total sales by $20,000. A three-hundred call firm that achieves a $400 average sales increase will augment total sales by $120,000.

EXHIBIT Q
TOTAL SALES INCREASE FROM A FULLY DEVELOPED MERCHANDISING PLAN-ALL PRODUCT CATEGORIES

		AVERAGE SALES INCREASE				
		$200	**$400**	**$600**	**$800**	**$1,000**
Number of Calls	**100**	20,000	40,000	60,000	80,000	100,000
	200	40,000	80,000	120,000	160,000	200,000
	300	60,000	120,000	180,000	240,000	300,000
	400	80,000	160,000	240,000	320,000	400,000
	500	100,000	200,000	300,000	400,000	500,000

What are the cash flow and profit possibilities resulting from such sales? That will depend, of course, on the incremental gross profit from the added sales and on the costs that are associated with changing your selection room and other display areas to a configuration that will achieve the added sales and the added gross profit. We will consider these factors one at a time.

Incremental Gross Profit

First, with regard to incremental gross profit. This is the dollar differential between total added sales and total added cost of goods sold.

Fortunately, funeral-related products enjoy generous markups which produce generous gross profits. What then, is the planned gross profit that we can anticipate from the added sales on a cumulative basis? To be ultraconservative, we'll use a cumulative markup of 2.0 times on incremental sales, which produces, of course, an incremental gross profit of 50%.

Substituting gross profit dollars for sales in the matrix table as shown in Exhibit R, we see that impressive increases in gross profit are possible also. A one-hundred call firm that achieves a $100 increase in average gross profit will augment total gross profit by $10,000 a year. A three-hundred call firm that achieves a $200 increase in average gross profit augment total gross profit by $60,000 a year.

EXHIBIT R
TOTAL GROSS PROFIT FROM A FULLY DEVELOPED MERCHANDISING PLAN—ALL PRODUCT CATEGORIES

		AVERAGE GROSS PROFIT INCREASE				
		$100	**$200**	**$300**	**$400**	**$500**
Number of Calls	**100**	10,000	20,000	30,000	40,000	50,000
	200	20,000	40,000	60,000	80,000	100,000
	300	30,000	60,000	90,000	120,000	150,000
	400	40,000	80,000	120,000	160,000	200,000
	500	50,000	100,000	150,000	200,000	250,000

Gross Profit to Net Profit

In funeral service, an increase in *incremental* gross profit, derived from a positive change in merchandise mix or from the sale of additional funeral-related products is just about equivalent to an increase in net profit. This is because *expenses do not tend to increase on a transaction basis* as a result of selling a better mix of products or from selling additional funeral-related products.[14]

[14]To the extent that funeral arrangers are compensated on a commission or bonus basis, there would be a differential between gross profit and net profit. These differences would still tend to be small, however.

Return on Investment

The true significance of the incremental profit numbers cannot be appreciated until they are related to the amount of investment that is needed to generate an increase in sales and increase in profit. When we do this, we find that the total additional investment is *moderate* and that the amortized cost of this investment on a yearly basis is *minuscule*. Further, since the programs invariably work, there is little financial risk involved.

As mentioned in the opening chapter of this book, in my thirty years of business and consulting experience, I have never encountered such dramatic and decisive returns.

It is this experience that prompted me to recall Winston Churchill's famous remark—"*Never have so many owed so much to so few.*" In funeral service, this can be paraphrased—"*Never has so much been accomplished with so little effort*" or—"*Never has there been such a profit return on so modest an investment*!"

Specifically, what are the investments that are required to develop a complete model stock program for all funeral product categories and to create a professional environment to display these products?

The investments are of three types: 1) inventory (at least for those products that are stocked as opposed to those sold from display samples); 2) the cost of new displays, fixtures, signs, equipment, lighting and physical environmental enhancements, and 3) where feasible, the cost of additional space—as might be planned into new buildings or into expansions.

From a balance sheet perspective, the first of these is an increase in current assets and the second and third are increases in fixed assets.

Inventory Investment

Let's consider inventory investment first. Quite obviously, if 10 to 20 caskets or urns are added to our assortment, these have to be financed from some source. And, since the additions are likely to be above-average units in wholesale value, such a decision could add $10,000 to $20,000 to the total amount invested in inventory.

To illustrate this point, let's add 15 caskets to our assortment at an average wholesale cost of $1,200 each. Let's also add 10 urns to our assortment at an average cost of $200 each. Together, this increase in caskets and urns adds $20,000 to our total inventory investment ($1,200 x 15 = $18,000; $200 x 10 = $2,000; $18,000 + $2,000 = $20,000).

In evaluating this increased investment, it is *essential* that we do not confuse it with an increase in cost of goods sold—even if it is so treated for accounting purposes. Many funeral homes, especially smaller funeral homes, treat all merchandise purchases as costs during the year in which they are purchased, disregarding beginning and ending inventories. This might be simple for bookkeeping purposes (and sometimes advantageous for tax purposes, if you can get away with it) but it *distorts* the business decision process.

In actuality, inventory is an asset. Caskets, urns and other merchandise purchased are items of absolute monetary value. If you were to sell your business, you would expect to receive payment for your inventory just as you would from buildings, equipment, furnishings, vehicles, and other assets.

Interestingly, in funeral service, inventory typically does not even lose value through depreciation. This is because when a funeral home owner or manager is dissatisfied with a particular item of merchandise, chances are he can get the supplier to take it back for full credit so long as it is replaced with another item by the same supplier. This is another way of saying that funeral homes—unlike many other businesses that buy and sell merchandise—do not have a problem with "shrinkage," which is the decline in value of inventory due to markdowns on slow-moving goods or inventory losses as a result of theft.

In summary, an increase in inventory investment is *not* an increase in the cost of the goods, per se. It only becomes a *cost* when an inventory item is *sold.*

In reality, the monetary expense of an increase in inventory is nothing more than the *loss in revenue* associated with money that might be invested elsewhere. At current interest rates, savings accounts are yielding approximately 3% before taxes. Long-term government bonds are yielding 6.0%. High quality corporate bonds are yielding 8 to 9%. A well-balanced portfolio of Blue Chip common stocks might yield 10 to 11% on a pre-tax basis, provided, of course, that you hold them over a long enough period of time.

As an alternative to disturbing existing investments, the money required for the new merchandising program could be borrowed. At today's interest rates, a well-managed funeral home with a respectable balance sheet could borrow funds at 7 to 8% from a commercial bank.[15]

But before we rush out and borrow $20,000 for the new merchandising program, it is necessary to distinguish between *total* inventory investment and *net* inventory investment. In actuality, we probably can install the merchandising program for considerably *less than* the $20,000, owing to the fact that some of the monies needed to finance the incremental inventory are provided to us free by our suppliers in the form of trade credit.

Let's take an example. Prior to the new merchandising program, let's say that our assortment consists of 20 caskets and 20 urns. The average wholesale cost of the caskets is

[15]Larger firms with very strong balance sheets could borrow funds at the prime rate or even at commercial paper rates that are less than prime.

$600 and the cost of the urns is $150. This amounts to an inventory investment of $12,000 for caskets ($600 x 20 = $12,000) and $3,000 for urns ($150 x 20 = $3,000). Our total dollar inventory investment, therefore, is $15,000 ($12,000 + $3,000 = $15,000).

In reviewing our accounts payables to casket and urn suppliers, we discover that *on the average*, we have an outstanding balance of about $5,000. This gives us a net inventory investment of two-thirds of the total or $10,000 ($15,000 - $5,000 = $10,000). This is the amount of the inventory that *our company* must fund from some other source—owners' money (net worth) or creditors' money (banks, insurance companies, or the like).

If the same ratio could be maintained with the new inventory investment, instead of having to fund $20,000, we would only have to fund $13,334, which is two-thirds of the total. In actuality, you might even be able to do better than this. The added inventory items—being more expensive on the average than those in the original assortment—are likely to turn more slowly than those in the original inventory. For this reason, you may be able to negotiate extended datings with your suppliers so that the $20,000 in additional inventory may require only a $10,000 net investment from you. Quite obviously, this is a matter of negotiation between each funeral home and its suppliers.

If the net inventory figure is $10,000, then we would calculate the cost of the additional inventory investment by determining the *loss in revenue* from the liquidation of some other investment or from the *cost of money* borrowed from some source to fund the investment. In order to be conservative, we will use the latter approach—borrowing from a bank at a market interest rate. For discussion purposes, let's say that this is 8%. This means that the new program will cost us $800 a year ($10,000 x .08% = $800) on a pre-tax basis.

In the final analysis, however, it is even *less than this* because interest charges are an *expense* for accounting and tax purposes. The actual out-of-pocket cost, therefore, is in the range of $500.[16]

Just think about what we have accomplished! We have almost doubled our assortment of caskets and urns—providing far greater choice to consumers—all for a net out-of-pocket inventory cost of $500 per year!

Clearly then, inventory investment cannot be an inhibiting factor in developing a fully-planned model stock assortment. The expense of the incremental inventory is really quite incidental. One sale of an above-average unit, otherwise not achieved, will more than pay for the interest expense on the inventory for an entire year!

Fixed Asset Investments

Once we have determined the true costs of our inventory investment, we can go to the next step and establish what it is going to cost to create the optimum environment for a full line of funeral-related products.

The word "optimum" has been chosen with care. As noted in Chapter 4, there is no single selection room configuration that is appropriate for all funeral homes around the country. Even the "state of the art" rooms need to be modified to fit individual circumstances of 1) space availability, 2) market demand, 3) supplier support availability, and 4) budget and return on investment considerations.

[16]The actual federal income tax rate will vary depending upon the type of corporation that you have. At this time, a regular corporation is taxed at a 35% rate; a subchapter "S" corporation is taxed as a proprietorship, with the marginal tax rate up to 39%. State and local income taxes, if any, must be considered in addition.

The Range of Possibilities

In deciding what you need to do to implement a total merchandising program, it is advisable to fit this program into your overall facilities plan. For example, if you are going to replace your existing funeral home with a new one in a year or two, you will want to develop a minimum budget plan in the short run. On the other hand, if you are going to build a new funeral home or substantially expand or remodel an existing one, it is easy to justify some version of a "state of the art" facility because the *marginal cost* of installing such a facility is quite modest when it is related to what you would be spending anyway. And, as noted throughout this book, no other investment in funeral service has been identified to produce anything like the return that can be produced through a total merchandising program.

Two Types of Fixed Asset Investments

There are two basic types of fixed assets used in connection with a total merchandising program: 1) display fixtures, signs, accent lighting and accessories, and 2) environmental enhancements, including ceilings, wall partitions, built-in lighting, wall surface materials and floor coverings.

While all of these costs will vary depending upon individual circumstances, there are now enough installations in place to relate the cost of each type of fixed asset investment to square footage considerations.

Display Fixtures, Signs, Accent Lighting and Accessories

Experience shows that it is practical to budget in the range of $10 to $15 per square foot for state of the art display fixtures, signs, accent lighting and decorative accessories. This would include double racks and upholstered pedestals for the casket selection room, special-purpose vault display units, bookcase-style cabinets for urns, and special-purpose display units for monuments and markers. It would also include a complete sign program including sign holders, uplights to "wash" the walls for special emphasis, spotlights to more effectively feature selected products, silk flowers and plants, and bronze and wood statues and pedestals.

Just as was the case with inventory investment, it is important to calculate these outlays on a *net* basis. Very often, key suppliers will bear a portion of these costs. In fact, some manufacturers will supply display fixtures for certain products on a complimentary basis. Care must be exercised, however, to be certain that such fixtures are compatible with the overall model stock assortment plan and the environmental plan.

Environmental Enhancements

The specific items typically included in environmental enhancements are: new ceilings, built-in electrical lighting fixtures, valances, niche partitions, trim and moldings, wall surfaces, and carpeting. The range of costs associated with these items varies from approximately $10 per square foot on the low side to $25 per square foot on the high side.

The significant variation in costs is explained by the different circumstances that are encountered from one funeral home to another. For example, an older funeral home might require a completely new ceiling and lighting installation whereas a newer home may not. A state of the art room might be fitted out with full-niche partitions—not only for caskets and vaults, but for flowers, clothing and other merchandise, whereas a somewhat less ambitious installation might be fitted out only with a valance around the perimeter of the room. A low-volume installation would require a carpet with less face weight of material than a high-volume firm, and so on.

Annualized Costs

By their very nature, if the investments described above are truly fixed assets, they have a life of many years. Therefore, we cannot confuse cash outlays for equipment or for environmental enhancements with yearly operating expenses. The annualized expense associated with these investments are: 1) the cost of funds associated with the investment, and 2) the depreciation cost associated with the gradual deterioration of the investment.

Let's assume a 1,000 square foot selection room where the useful life of the equipment is five years and that the useful life of the environmental enhancements is ten years. Let's further assume that our cash outlay for equipment is $10,000 and for environmental enhancements is $16,000. Our annualized cost, based upon this rate of depreciation is:

Display fixtures, signs, accent lighting, accessories (net)*
($10,000 ÷ 5 = $2,000)..$2,000

Environmental enhancements (net)*
($16,000 ÷ 10 = $1,600)..1,600

TOTAL..$3,600

*The "net" cost to the funeral home after supplier participation.

In order to arrive at total cost, we must add to this all interest charges for the funds used in connection with the installation. To be technically correct, this number will reduce each year, if you use the depreciation to pay off the capital balance of the term loan that you have taken out to pay for the installation. However, in order to be ultra-conservative, we will use the cost of funds in the first year of the installation, when interest costs will be at their highest. As was the case for the inventory investment, let's assume that we borrow money from our bank at 8% interest. This gives us a carrying cost of $2,080 ($26,000 x .08% = $2,080) for the first year of the installation.

Based upon the above, we can summarize the total cost of the installation as follows:

1. Depreciation on display fixtures, signs, accent lighting, etc. (net)*:
   $10,000 ÷ 5 = $2,000 .... $2,000

2. Depreciation on environmental enhancements:
   $16,000 ÷ 10 = $1,600 1,600

3. Cost of capital:
   a. Inventory investment (net)*
      $10,000 x .08 = $800 800
   b. Display fixtures, etc. (net)*
      $10,000 x .08 = $800 800
   c. Environmental enhancements
      $16,000 x .08 = $1,280 1,280

TOTAL COST BEFORE TAXES $6,480

*The "net" cost to the funeral home after supplier participation.

Realized Return on Investment

We are now ready to relate the total annualized cost of the advanced merchandising program to the anticipated profit return from the program. Referring back to Exhibit R, let's take a one-hundred call firm that generates a $200 incremental gross profit for a total profit increase of $20,000 per year. When we subtract our total cost of $6,480 from that return, we produce an incremental profit of $13,520 ($20,000 -$6,480 = $13,520). Our return on investment in the first year is 208.6% ($13,520 ÷ $6,480 = 208.6%). Our return in subsequent years would be *higher* owing to the fact that interest charges would be lower.

This is the return using a very conservative set of assumptions. If we were to assume a $300 incremental gross profit return per call, our total profit increases to $23,520 per year. If we assume a $400 increase, our total profit goes to $33,520 per year. Our return on investment, therefore, becomes: at $300 per call ($23,520 - $6,480 = $17,040 ÷ $6,480 = 263.0%); at $400 per call ($33,520 - $6,480 = $27,040 ÷ $6,480 = 417.2%).

These are truly conservative goals based upon actual field experience with various aspects of this type of program. Clearly, when we achieve results at these levels, the return on investment is spectacular by any yardstick.

CHAPTER 6

FUNERAL SERVICE IN THE YEAR 2000

The best way to predict the future is create it!

—Tom Peters

Destiny is not a matter of chance; it is a matter of choice.

—William Jennings Bryan

As stated at the outset, funeral home owners and managers view themselves primarily as professional service providers, not as merchandising specialists. This is as it should be—the service side of the business clearly is of paramount importance. The merchandising side plays the supporting role.

Contemporary Professional Practice

But the true *professional* today—in every field—appreciates that the body of knowledge needed to practice as a professional is broadly based. Many of the breakthroughs that are taking place are coming from "outside" of the narrow confines of the "traditional" body of knowledge. Hence, the field of medicine is being revolutionized by electronic scanning, laser surgery, biochemical formulations, and the like. The practice of law is being transformed by the technology of computerized databases, telecommunications, desktop publishing, and next day air express.

So it is with the professional practice of funeral service. It is being transformed by new knowledge about model stock assortment planning, pricing, display, fixturing, merchandise presentation, lighting, and environmental design.

But the new knowledge does not stop there. It goes further and impacts other aspects of funeral service. It involves a knowledge of real estate location theory, new concepts of total funeral home planning—especially energy efficient "smart" buildings, new funeral home layouts, and new interior designs—computerized accounting and information systems, new interpretations of "customer service" and, certainly an appreciation for changing *employee* and *consumer* attitudes and values.

The true professional funeral home owner and manager will use all of the above knowledge to reinvent the very nature and essence of funeral service for the twenty-first century. But none will do it independently. Suppliers and outside service organizations will play a major role in synthesizing the knowledge so that it can be used practically. Professional schools, trade associations, and information exchange groups will play an important part in documenting case studies of firms that are successfully applying the new knowledge.

For those who view change positively, it is going to be a rewarding time to be in funeral service. The business will be different, but it will be more interesting because reinvent-ors will create more value for consumers, for employees, and for stockholders *simultaneously.*

How is this possible? Is this not a contradiction in terms? Does not giving more value to consumers mean lower prices and therefore lower profits? Does not giving greater benefits to employees mean higher expenses and therefore lower profits?

This is the case *only* if you think in outmoded paradigms! Only if you define value as synonymous with price.

Make no mistake about it, price is important. Funeral directors need to be sensitive to having a reputation of being "high priced." And certainly they need to be sensitive to the perception held by certain social critics and media guru's that the funeral industry "gouges the public."

There is a straightforward way to counter such negative publicity. It is to make certain that it is *not* true! It is to make certain that your total service and product offer meets or surpasses the *changing expectations of your customers.* Not your traditional expectations, not those of your employees, but your customers!

Customer Expectations in the 1990s

Chances are that these expectations already are quite different than your perceptions of what they are. Funeral directors, as a whole, still have a tendency to think in terms of traditional funerals (preferred) on the one hand and cremations (when demanded) on the other. In actuality, the service and product offer that is needed today already is much more complicated than this, and by the year 2000, it is going to be enormously more complicated still.

The same knowledge, experience and information that is available to the consumer to demand quality automobiles for example—in an almost infinite variety of makes and models—is going to cause the consumer to demand a quality assortment of funeral-related products.

And the same knowledge, experience and information that is causing the consumer to demand quality automotive *service*—in an almost infinite number of variations—is going to cause the consumer to demand more complete and more imaginative funeral service—in an almost infinite number of variations.

Isn't it interesting that consumers have ranked the Lexus as the No. 1 automobile in product quality and service in the J.D. Power annual survey of customer satisfaction for the last three years in a row? Not Mercedes Benz, BMW, Cadillac, Jaguar, or other venerable nameplates, but a totally new product sold by a totally new dealer organization! Some of the other prestige names mentioned did not even rank in the Top Ten.

How could such a thing happen? You know the answer—Lexus created a product/service offer that gives consumers *superior value*. What is even more interesting is the speed at which consumers *perceived* this value.

This is not, incidentally, a high end or "carriage trade" phenomenon. Acura accomplished the same thing in the middle-priced automobile market in the late 1980s and Chrysler appears to be doing it at this time. Honda has captured the superior value image in the lower-priced market just as Volkswagen did a generation earlier.

Creating Enduring Value

The Honda story is particularly enlightening in helping us understand how to create *enduring value.*

George Gilder, in his provocative book, *The Spirit of Enterprise,* compares the American-made Chevrolet Chevette with the Japanese-made Honda Civic, circa 1975.[17] He points out that the gross weight of the two vehicles was practically identical and that the amount of metal, rubber, glass, plastic, chrome and textiles used in the vehicles was—pound for pound—almost the same, as was the cost of these materials.

The Honda Civic, as you no doubt know, developed a reputation of being a very dependable and economical car. It was in great demand. For hundreds of thousands of young people in America, it was their "first" car. The Civic provided the cash flow for Honda to develop an even more powerful product—the Accord—which subsequently became the best selling car in America.[18]

The Chevrolet Chevette, regrettably for General Motors and for America in general, was representative of much of the shoddy output of the country in the 1970s and 1980s. Because of its basic flaws—poor quality, poor performance, and a poor record of reliability—the car became a source of ridicule. Consumer activists, automotive magazine editors, and user surveys were almost unanimous in their disdain for the vehicle. Not surprisingly, the Chevette depreciated quickly and consumers bought them only at distressed

[17]George Gilder. *The Spirit of Enterprise.* (Simon and Schuster: New York, 1984) pp. 194-197.

[18]The Honda Accord was the No. 1 selling car in American in 1989, 1990, and 1991. In 1992, the Accord took second place to the Ford Taurus. However, examination of the sale data shows that the Taurus was No. 1 as a result of its "fleet" sales to the rent-a-car industry. Without the addition of fleet sales, the Accord would have continued to be the No. 1 seller in 1992.

Motors was forced to withdraw the car from the market in the mid-1980s.[19]

Why did the Honda Civic capture the imagination of so many people in the American market? Why did the Chevrolet Chevette become the source of ridicule? It is because one company provided a superior total offer—product and service—at a fair price (which, incidentally, was higher than the Chevette) and the other company did not. One company was committed to the concept of *creating enduring value* and the other company was out to make a fast buck.

But the real difference between the Honda Civic and the Chevrolet Chevette was not even in the product, per se. It was in the business *attitudes* and *values* of the leaders who were running the companies. These values are the important ones because they make it possible to create superior organizations which, in turn, develop superior people which in turn, create superior products and services.

Honda, under the guidance of its inspirational founder, Soichiro Honda, had dedicated itself to designing, manufacturing, marketing and servicing a line of cars that were *as good as they could be*! General Motors unfortunately, had no such similar philosophy. In fact, it is probably reasonable to state that the very notion of building any Chevrolet "as good as it could be" was alien to the prevailing positioning strategy of trading up customers from Chevrolet to Pontiac to Buick to Oldsmobile to Cadillac.

[19]Unfortunately, this was not the only ill-conceived vehicle produced by General Motors during this period. The Cadillac Cimarron suffered a similar fate. It was nothing more than a dressed up Chevrolet Cavalier compact selling at a high price. The American public was not to be duped. They simply refused to buy the car and it too, had to be withdrawn from the market. Automotive experts are united in their opinion that this car did irreparable damage to the name and reputation of Cadillac.

On this subject, I am able to speak from personal experience. During the 1980s, I was heavily involved as a marketing consultant to the automotive industry. I was from this perspective that I was able to write *Reinventing the Wheels: Ford's Spectacular Comeback*. Essentially, this is a book about how an American company changed its *ethos*; its *fundamental beliefs, customs and practices*. This was required *before* the company could make any sense out of the idea that "Quality is Job No. 1" at Ford. As a point in fact, Ford had been on many quality campaigns in the past, but none of them had worked. The same was true of General Motors. During the 1970s, GM embarked upon its highly publicized "Mark of Excellence" program, but this is the same company that produced in the same decade, the Chevrolet Chevette and the Cadillac Cimarron.

Creating Enduring Value in Funeral Service

Reinventing Funeral Service is not about merchandising for merchandising's sake. It is not about making money for the sake of making money. And it's certainly *not* about how to get rich quick by taking advantage of the consumer.

It is about generating the cash flow to provide the wherewithal to serve consumers more creatively, employees more adequately, and owners more advantageously. It is about generating higher profits in the long term because funeral home owners and managers have redefined their service and product offers to be more in tune with what the American public needs and wants.

It is about providing more, rather than less. But not more in terms of a narrow, obsolete view of a physical product. In funeral service much is made about the concept of a funeral home's *merchandise value ratio* or it's MVR. This proposition postulates that a casket sale that is a certain percentage of the funeral total sale (approaching 20%) is somehow "good" and one which falls substantially below this is somehow taking advantage of the consumer.

This concept is based upon spurious logic. It is like saying that ordering a 20-ounce steak in a restaurant is better than ordering a 14-ounce steak. Clearly, one is not necessarily better than the other. It depends upon the circumstances. And, with what we now know about nutrition, there may be good reasons not to order the larger steak.

In this field also, I speak with some personal experience as I have investment interests in two different restaurant companies. One of these companies operates with a 30% food cost, while the other operates with a 40% food cost. Yet, the company with the 30% food cost does considerably more volume than the one with the 40% food cost. This suggests that something *other than* food cost as a percentage of sales (MVR) is important in the equation.

In reality, these businesses operate quite differently. The one with the lower food cost has a creative and expansive menu. It operates with a very talented chef and a large kitchen staff. Many of the items on the menu are created "from scratch." The other is a grill-style restaurant with a more limited menu of prime steaks, chops, and fresh seafood. It operates with a higher food cost, but with a more limited kitchen staff. Interestingly, when food cost and kitchen labor cost are added together in both restaurants, they have about the same overall cost percentage of 60%.

It isn't that one restaurant company is *better* than the other intrinsically. As a matter of fact, both receive the highest ratings in their class. Both are highly profitable and both have net profit margins which approach 20% pre-tax—not unlike those achieved by well-run funeral homes.

Are these businesses charging too much? They certainly aren't inexpensive. The average check size at one is $28 and at the other it is $31 per person. Yet both businesses have more customers each year and higher sales each year.

Why? It is because the customers who patronize these restaurants feel that they are receiving *true value*. These restaurants are quality *experiences.* Quality as defined in terms of food taste and presentation (not mere quantity), personal attention by the staff, and superior ambience. Quality in little things—from the moment you arrive in your car and are greeted by the parking attendant to the moment you leave and are thanked by the manager on duty for your patronage.

And so it must be with funeral service. It is not about the merchandising of products in and of themselves. It is not about embalming, or about providing "traditional" service. It is not even about "funerals" as we have traditionally known them.

The Changing Nature of Funeral Service

Funeral service in the year 2000 is about getting in touch with the attitudes and values of people. It is more and more about the celebration of long life, and about the helping of people at the end of life. And, this includes arrangements for people who are dealing with the end of *their own* lives. It is about honor, dignity, love, respect, memories, and humor. It is about faith, religion, ritual, music, homily, ceremony and procession. It is about beautiful and tasteful surroundings and appropriate amenities. It is about remembrance and memorialization.

It is about putting all of the services and the products that are associated with funeral service into *context.* It is about preserving the best of tradition and abandoning the excess or the out of date.

This starts with a redefinition of the word *service.* Too many funeral directors perhaps confuse "empathy" with "service."

Indeed, funeral directors as a whole, are very sensitive to the needs of families at a time when they are under considerable stress and in emotional turmoil. But even in this area, there is a need for change. There certainly is the need to avoid the tendency, still widely observed in the industry, of talking and behaving in an unctuous manner. It is this excessive piousness and moralistic fervor—so often portrayed in motion pictures as the stereotypical funeral director—that helps to give the industry a bad name.

More importantly, there is the need to abandon the dichotomy of viewing funerals as "traditional services" on the one hand and "cremation services" on the other. In the future, there will be the need for many different types of service, including a large number of customized or individualized services.

Individualized preferences begin with convenience —convenience of location, convenience of arrangements, convenience of scheduling, and convenience of the funeral service itself. This suggests that funeral home owners and managers are going to have to look objectively at their physical facilities.

There will be a need for formal services and informal services, elegant services and simple services, solemn services and casual services, long services and short services, open-casket services (and, therefore, traditional embalming) and closed-casket services (sometimes without embalming) and, more and more, individualized services. As one astute funeral director exclaimed, "We already are providing customized services—all you have to do is look at your pre-need write-ups and you'll see just how strong individualized preferences have become."

The important action plan is to embrace these changes *positively,* rather than reacting passively or negatively to them—as many funeral directors have done for years with regard to cremation services. Even today, many funeral home owners and managers think of cremation as a low margin type of limited service, rather than what it really is—an opportunity to provide a variety of services (and products) to families that have a preference for this method of disposal.[20]

I will never forget the story told to me by my funeral director friend, Charlie Farmer, from Springdale, Arkansas. It is about a cremation and cemetery interment that he arranged for the wife and family of a retired paratrooper. This particular family expressed to the funeral director, in no uncertain terms, that they were not interested in any aspect of a traditional funeral service—embalming, casketing, viewing, prayer services, church services, or the like. There were interested in cremation and cemetery interment only.

In talking further with the family, however, Charlie discovered that the U.S. Army Paratroop Corps was a very important aspect of the life of the deceased as well as the family of the deceased. He asked the family if they might like to recognize this in some way at the cemetery. While they were at a loss as to what to do, they responded positively to the idea. Charlie, on his own, arranged for an army reservist to parachute from a plane, in full uniform, to within 25 feet of the gravesite at the exact time of the interment. After landing, the paratrooper went over to the gravesite, saluted, then walked up to the family, saluted a second time, and presented the wife with the American flag!

This service was not performed gratuitously. In fact, an appropriate fee was charged for making these special arrangements. But not surprisingly, the family was so moved by the experience that no mention was made of the cost of the service.

[20]Michael W. Kubasak. *Cremation and the Funeral Director: Successfully Meeting the Challenge*. (Malibu, California: The Avalon Press, 1990).

And had there been—it would have been no problem because Charlie Farmer was in a position to write off the expense without worrying about it for a minute. As it turned out, the positive publicity and the word of mouth value of the event would have made it more than worthwhile anyway.

Interestingly, modern technology will *greatly augment* the possibilities of arranging for more individualized services and memorializations. We see this already with video cassette programming. But this is only the tip of the iceberg. Electronic programming is being developed which will allow for an almost limitless offer of choral and instrumental musical accompaniment—supporting individualized consumer preferences for solemn versus casual services, or what have you. This technology will allow the funeral director to simulate the sound and the order of worship of the great choirs and churches in the world or the sounds of the most popular artists of the time. Modern lighting technology also will enhance the beauty and serenity of such services.

The overriding concept is that successful funeral homes in the future are going to provide *more service* rather than *less service.* The "more" may be in the form of more convenient locations—closer to where consumers are living or on cemetery grounds, providing for a completely different type of "one stop" convenience that is desirable in the hustle-bustle of modern life.

The "more" may be in the form of more complete or attractive facilities—that provide for more privacy, more esthetic surroundings, more beautiful chapels, or more amenities such as private dining rooms, lounges, or the like.

In my view, another volume needs to be written on the characteristics of the funeral home of the future and I plan to write such a book next year. Suffice it to say here that such facilities will epitomize the "more for less" principle—they will be built to greatly enhance customer satisfaction and, at the same time, they will be more efficient to operate—from an energy point of view and an employee staffing point of view. Few funeral home owners now realize that energy savings and payroll savings alone from a well-planned modern facility ***can pay for an entire new facility over the depreciated life of the facility***! And with interest rates at historic lows, this is more the case than ever.

When this awareness is combined with the awareness of the benefits of state of the art merchandising programs, more and more funeral home owners, no doubt, will be building such facilities.

"More" service will be performed by better selected, better trained, and better compensated funeral directors and support staff personnel. Better selected, because modern testing techniques will aid in the selection process. Better trained, because modern seminars and training programs (many of which will be on video cassettes and on laser disks) will be used to advance the technical skills and the people skills of key employees. Better compensated because the "economics" of funeral service will provide for it—through more profitable service sales and more profitable product sales.

Last but not least, funeral service in the year 2000 will be orchestrated by more imaginative, energetic and enlightened funeral home owners—who are confident of their mission to serve the public in the most creative, responsible and satisfying way possible.

EPILOGUE

During the development of this book, I happened to discuss its contents with an old friend, Étienne Thil, a leading French marketing consultant. Étienne subsequently sent me a dossier on Roc Eclerc, a Paris-headquartered company that had challenged in the courts the well-entrenched, almost monopoly position of the "PFG" (les Pompes Funébres Générales), the state-sanctioned official association of funeral establishments in France.

I particularly remembered an article entitled, "La Mort en Discount," which described how Roc Eclerc was selling funeral products and services at a discount in a "supermarket" configuration, even employing a self-service, checkout technique for some products. While this seemed farfetched, my consulting experience in France over many years prompted me not to dismiss this outright, as the French are far and away the most innovative retailers in Europe.

It was on a trip to France in October 1993 that I visited Roc Eclerc for the first time. I could hardly believe my eyes! Here was a 10,000-square-foot *retail store* selling an entire range of funeral products and services—at prices claimed to be 30% to 40% below those charged by the PFG and its affiliates.

I will describe my visit to this facility in detail. It was located in Creteil, a suburb of Paris. It was, in fact, a retail store with large signs on the exterior of the building and plate glass windows so that it was possible to see the merchandise on display inside the store. Upon entering—behind the checkout counter—was the flower and plant department consisting of more than 100 live and artificial arrangements. These ranged from small sizes up to huge funeral sprays 5 to 6 feet in height.

Next was the monument department (an obviously important part of the total business) with a selection of approximately two dozen full-sized marble and granite edifices—in the European style of an upright headpiece (about 4 x 4 feet in size) and an ornamental grave cover (about 4 x 8 feet in size).

Following this was the memorial placard and accessories department, which consisted of several hundred different memorial pieces (approximately 1 x 1 foot in size) made from marble, granite, glass, ceramic materials, and lucite. There was an elaborate display showing how these could be customized including etching the face of the deceased upon the surface of the placard.

The casket showroom was off to the side, but still a part of the retail store. It showed approximately 20 wooden caskets made from different specie and finished to different levels of sophistication. The caskets were displayed upright and, from a distance, looked like a large assortment of Grandfather clocks. Interiors and casket hardware were sold and displayed separately, in different colors, materials and designs, with the opportunity for the consumer to choose any interior or any style of hardware to be fitted to any casket.

Funeral arrangements were made from semiprivate offices at the rear of the store, much like would be found in an American automobile dealership. Metal and glass partitions separated the offices and printed lists depicting different funeral packages were displayed from the partitions.

The overall impression—from a North American perspective—was quite shocking. Nothing about the facility was very subtle and the straightforward, almost blatant, presentation of goods and services took some getting used to.

Yet, here was a business already putting into practice—albeit in extreme form—the principles which I have put forth in this book! And, they are working incredibly well.

I found out that the first Roć Eclerc "Supermarché Du Funéraire" opened in December 1991, but that subsequently—in less than two years—51 additional stores have been opened—each in excess of 5,000 square feet. Four of the stores are company owned and 48 are franchised outlets. Fifty of the stores are in France; one is in Belgium and the other is in Switzerland.

Clearly, based upon this growth rate something quite important was going on, so I decided to remain in Paris an extra day in order to meet personally with Michel LeClerc, chairman and founder of the company. I spent the better part of a day with Messieur LeClerc and his top management staff. They were very gracious in their hospitality and very open and candid about their plans to revolutionize funeral practices in Europe.

I further discovered that Michel LeClerc was not new to retailing innovations. His brother, Edouard, was a pioneering supermarket and hypermarket operator in France and Michel himself had been a pioneer in new methods of automotive and gasoline service retailing.

He founded Roć Eclerc almost ten years ago, convinced that the state monopoly system granting exclusive geographical territories to funeral home operators was not in the consumer's interest. He was convinced that the consumer had little choice in the product or the service side of what was being offered and that prices were too high.

His first step was to recruit licensed funeral home operators who would agree to work with him in an arrangement outside of the PFG, and who would agree to sell at lower prices. This turned out to be a national controversy with the PFG fighting vigorously to maintain its privileged position. Altogether, some 1,800 lawsuits were filed against Roć Eclerc over an eight-year period, but the company prevailed on December 23, 1992, when the French National Assembly ruled that the PFG system could no longer monopolize funeral service in the country.

Free from the restrictions and expense of defending hundreds of lawsuits simultaneously, the company was poised for rapid growth. At present, there are almost 300 affiliated outlets in addition to the superstore outlets. These outlets together handle over 100,000 funerals a year which represents 18 percent of all deaths in France.

The supermarket stores range in size from 5,000 square feet to 15,000 square feet. Inventory investment is approximately $200,000 and the fitting out investment is approximately $100,000 (excluding real estate and building costs).

The original store opened in December 1991. It is now doing more than $6,000,000 (in U.S. dollars) in volume annually. The concept is so new that it is too early to ascertain the sales volume of the average store, but Michel LeClerc feels that it would be in the range of $3,000,000 per year, with two-thirds of the total business coming from product sales and one-third from service sales.

There are many cultural differences between funeral practices in Europe and those in North America and there are also differences in the competitive structure of funeral service businesses that serve these markets. The purpose of this epilogue is to report on the Roć Eclerc formula, not to endorse it. I do not know the extent to which it will revolutionize funeral practices in Europe, let alone have any influence in the United States, Canada, or Mexico. The concept is still quite new and the competitive response from established operators has not yet been defined.

Nevertheless, the development is a stark reminder that consumers will *respond quickly* and *decisively* to businesses that offer them superior products and/or services at more favorable prices. In short, businesses that create more *value* for consumers.

I discussed this development at length with my friend, Étienne Thil. He mentioned to me that the French language does not have a word that is precisely equivalent to the word "value" as it is used in the English language. Etienne went on to say that this was quite regrettable because the word "value" was such a perfect expression to delineate the essence of what a modern business must provide for its customers.

I have written this entire book out of the conviction that funeral homes—around the world—must create *contemporary* values for today's consumers, today's employees, and for tomorrow's owners.

—AFD

ABOUT THE AUTHOR

Alton F. Doody, Jr., began his consulting practice in 1964. His clients have included consumer goods manufacturers and retailers throughout the world.

He earned a B.A. in 1956 from Ohio Wesleyan University, an M.B.A. in 1957, and a Ph.D. in 1961 from The Ohio State University, where he was a Professor of Marketing until 1972. He left full-time teaching to concentrate on his consulting practice and to pursue private investments.

Doody is co-author of *Retailing Management*, and more recently, *Reinventing the Wheels: Ford's Spectacular Comeback*. He is also the author of articles for *The Harvard Business Review*, *The Journal of Marketing*, *The Encyclopedia Britannica*, and others.

He is a co-founder of Management Horizons, Inc., a marketing consulting firm that is now a division of Price-Waterhouse. He is the founder of Retail Planning Associates and co-founder of Applied Retail Systems, both with headquarters in Columbus, Ohio. He is also founder and Chairman of The Doody Group with offices in New Orleans, Louisiana.

Doody's involvement in funeral service began in 1987. He first developed—in association with the Batesville Casket Company—new approaches to merchandise assortment planning, pricing, fixturing, display, and selection room design. More recently, in association with The Doody Group, he has pioneered new approaches to total funeral home planning and design, with projects completed for Stewart Enterprises, SCI, The Sentinel Group, and leading independent firms in the industry.

Awards received by Alton F. Doody, Jr., include the Founder's Award for Distinguished Service, Ohio Wesleyan University in 1989; Marketing Man of the Year Award from the American Marketing Association in 1980; the Outstanding Teacher Award from The Ohio State University in 1972, and the Wholesaler of the Year Award presented jointly by the National Hardware Manufacturers Association and the National Wholesale Hardware Association in 1970.

He serves as a director of The Newell Company, Grant Investments, Inc., Hyde Park Restaurants, Inc., Pet People Inc., Applied Retail Systems, Inc., and The Doody Group, Inc. He is a Senior Fellow at The A.B. Freeman School of Business, Tulane University, and a member of the Dean's Advisory Council. He is Captain of New Orleans' oldest Mardi Gras night parading organization.

Earlier in his career, Doody served as a First Lieutenant, United States Air Force, as a Trustee of Ohio Wesleyan University and of The Center of Science and Industry, Columbus, Ohio. He has been an active member of The Young Presidents Organization.

He is a native of New Orleans, Louisiana and is married to Elizabeth Hendrickson and has four children. Dr. and Mrs. Doody reside in New Orleans, Louisiana in the winter and Petoskey, Michigan in the summer.

SELECTED REFERENCES

Anderson, Patricia. *Affairs in Order: A Complete Resource Guide to Death and Dying.* (New York, New York: Macmillan Publishing Company).

Aries, P. *Western Attitudes Toward Death: From the Middle Ages to the Present.* (Baltimore, Maryland: The Johns Hopkins University Press, 1974).

Barker, Joel Arthur, *Paradigms: The Business of Discovering the Future.* New York, New York: HarperCollins Publishers, Inc., 1992).

Bowman, LeRoy. *The American Funeral: A Study in Guilt, Extravagance, and Sublimity.* (Washington, D.C.: Public Affairs Press, 1959).

Bradley, Buff. *ENDINGS: A Book About Death.* (Reading, Massachusetts: Addison-Wesley Publishing Company, Inc., 1979).

Brauchli, Marcus W. "Columbarium Owner Finds Cash Can Cure Local Fear of Ghosts." *The Wall Street Journal*, November 17, 1992.

Coffin, Margaret. *Death in Early America: The History and Folklore of Customs and Superstitions of Early Medicine, Funerals, Burials, and Mourning.* (Nashville, Tennessee, 1976).

Davidson, William R., Doody, Alton F., and Sweeney, Daniel J. *Retailing Management.* Fourth Edition. (New York, New York: John Wiley & Sons, 1975).

Davidow, William H. and Malone, Michael S. *The Virtual Corporation.* (New York, New York: HarperCollins Publishers, Inc., 1992).

DeSpelder, L.A. and Strickland, A.L. *The Last Dance: Encountering Death and Dying.* (Palo Alto, California: Mayfield Publishing Company, 1983).

Doody, Alton F. and Bingaman, Ron. *Reinventing the Wheels: Ford's Spectacular Comeback.* (Cambridge, Massachusetts: Ballinger Publishing Company, 1988).

Drucker, Peter F. *Managing for Results.* (New York, New York: Harper & Row, 1986).

_____________. *Management: Tasks, Responsibilities, Practices.* (New York, New York: Harper & Row, 1985).

_____________. *Post-Capitalist Society.* (New York, New York: HarperCollins Publishers, Inc., 1993).

Gerber, J., Wolff, J., Klores, W., and Brown, G. *Lifetrends: The Future of Baby Boomers and Other Aging Americans.* (New York, New York: Macmillan Publishing Company, 1989).

Gilder, George. *The Spirit of Enterprise* (Simon & Schuster: New York, 1984).

Habenstein, Robert W. and Lamers, William. *Funeral Customs the World Over.* (Milwaukee, Wisconsin: The National Funeral Directors Association of the United States, 1974).

_____________. *History of American Funeral Directing.* (Milwaukee, Wisconsin: National Funeral Directors of the United States, 1955, 1962, 1981).

Hammer, Michael and Champy, James. *Reengineering the Corporation: A Manifesto for Business Revolution.* (New York, New York: HarperCollins Publishers, Inc., 1993).

Harmer, Ruth Mulvey. *The High Cost of Dying.* (New York, New York: Collier Books, 1963).

Irion, Paul E. *The Funeral: Vestige or Value?* (Nashville, Tennessee: Parthenon Press, 1966).

Jackson, Charles O. *Passing: The Vision of Death in America.* (Westport, Connecticut: Greenwood Press, 1977).

Kubasak, Michael W. *Cremation and the Funeral Director: Successfully Meeting the Challenge.* (Malibu, California: The Avalon Press, 1990).

Kübler-Ross, Elisabeth. *Death: The Final Stage of Growth.* (Englewood Cliffs, New Jersey: Prentice-Hall, Inc., 1975).

___________. *On Death and Dying.* (New York, New York, Macmillan Publishing Company, 1969).

Liswood, Laura A. *Serving Them Right.* (New York, New York: Harper & Row, Publishers, 1990).

Longino, Jr., C.F., and Crown, W. H. "Older Americans." *American Demographics*, August, 1991.

Menchen, Robert. *The Last Caprice*. (New York, New York: Simon & Schuster, 1963).

Mitford, Jessica. *The American Way of Death.* (Greenwich, Connecticut: Fawcett Publications, Inc., 1963).

Morgan, Ernest. Dealing *Creatively with Death: A Manual of Death Education and Simple Burial.* (Bayside, New York: Barclay House, 1990).

Moschis, George P. "Marketing to Older Adults." *The Journal of Consumer Marketing*, Vol. 8, No. 4, Fall, 1991.

Nelson, Thomas C. *It's Your Choice: The Practical Guide to Planning a Funeral.* (Glenview, Illinois: Scott, Foresman and Company, 1983).

Newcomer, Stephen K. *Merchandising Through Product Knowledge: Niche Marketing in the Nineties.* Presentation: The Arkansas Funeral Directors Association State Convention, Hot Springs, Arkansas, June 30, 1993.

Osborne, David and Gaebler, T. *Reinventing Government: How the Entrepreneurial Spirit is Transforming the Public Sector.* (Reading, Massachusetts: Addison-Wesley Publishing Company, 1992).

Peck, Scott. *The Different Drum: Community Making and Peace.* (New York, New York: Simon & Schuster, 1987).

Popcorn, Faith. *The Popcorn Report.* (New York, New York: HarperCollins Publishers, Inc., 1991, 1992).

Raether, Howard C. *Funeral Service: A Historical Perspective.* (National Funeral Directors Association, 1990).

Shneidman, Edwin S. *Death: Current Perspectives.* (Palo Alto, California: Mayfield Publishing Company, 1976).

Stannard, David E. *The Puritan Way of Death: A Study in Religion, Culture, and Social Change.* (New York, New York: The Oxford University Press, 1977).

Veatch, Robert M. *Death, Dying, and the Biological Revolution: Our Last Quest for Responsibility.* (Cambridge, Massachusetts: Shenkman Publishing Company, 1977).

Whiteley, Richard C. *The Customer-Driven Company: Moving from Talk to Action.* (Reading, Massachusetts: Additon-Wesley Publishing Company, Inc., 1991).

Womack, James P., Jones, Daniel T., Roos, D., and Carpenter, D.S. *The Machine That Changed the World.* (New York, New York: Macmillan Publishing Company, 1990).

INDEX